DISCARD

You Can't Read This

You Can't Read This

Forbidden Books,
Lost Writing,
Mistranslations & Codes

VAL ROSS

Tundra Books

Published in Canada by Tundra Books,
75 Sherbourne Street, Toronto, Ontario M5A 2P9

Published in the United States by Tundra Books of Northern New York,
P.O. Box 1030, Plattsburgh, New York 12901

Library of Congress Control Number: 2005927015

Library and Archives Canada Cataloguing in Publication

Ross, Val
You can't read this : forbidden books, lost writing, mistranslations,
and codes / Val Ross.

Includes index.
ISBN 13: 978-0-88776-732-6
ISBN 10: 0-88776-732-X

1. Books and reading – History – Juvenile literature.
2. Reading – History – Juvenile literature. I. Title.

Z1003.R75 2006   j028'.09   C2005-904164-1

We acknowledge the financial support of the Government of Canada through the
Book Publishing Industry Development Program (BPIDP) and that of the Government of
Ontario through the Ontario Media Development Corporation's Ontario Book Initiative.
We further acknowledge the support of the Canada Council for the Arts
and the Ontario Arts Council for our publishing program.

ONTARIO ARTS COUNCIL
CONSEIL DES ARTS DE L'ONTARIO

Typeset in Goudy
Design: Terri Nimmo

Printed and bound in Canada

1   2   3   4   5   6   11   10   09   08   07   06

To those I walk with,
and to the three Morton and I watched
as they learned to walk

Contents

Introduction — I

1 The First Readers — 4

2 Language Lost and Language Found — 8

3 The Poet and the Emperor — 18

4 The Made-to-Order Alphabet — 25

5 The Prayerful Pagodas — 31

6 The Stolen Story — 34

7 The Pillage of Baghdad — 38

8 Giving Books to the People — 45

9 Darkness upon the Deep — 55

10 The Cousins and the Code — 62

11 Books Not to be Read — 67

12	That Dreadful Mr. Shakespeare	73
13	A Book at His Fingertips	81
14	Freddy the Slave Boy	87
15	The Two-Faced Treaty	94
16	The Evil World of – Comic Books?	101
17	Days of the Taliban	112
18	Access Denied	119
	Source Notes	126
	Picture Notes	132
	Acknowledgments	135
	Index	137

You Can't Read This

Introduction

WHEREVER PEOPLE CAN read, there are stories about the magic, mystery, and power of what they read. Because reading unlocks knowledge and power, people hoard it and fight for it just as they fight for treasures and gold.

The ancient Romans told a tale about one of their kings, Tarquin, who wanted to know what fate had in store for his kingdom so that he could be a better, stronger ruler. He went to see the Sibyl of Cumae, a wise woman who lived in a cave, to ask her to read the future. As the king approached the dark cavern, the old woman looked up from where she huddled by a fire and told him that all the future was written in her own nine books of prophecy. She said she would sell these books to him – for a very high price.

King Tarquin laughed angrily at the outrageous amount. "Ridiculous," he said. "I'd never pay that."

"Very well," said the Sibyl. She threw three of her nine books into the fire.

"But what part of the future was that?" said the alarmed king.

"Whatever it was, it is now unknowable," the Sibyl replied. "Do you want the other six books?"

This version of the Sibyl of Cumae was painted in the early 1600s by Domenico Zampieri, an artist who worked mostly in Rome and Naples. The sybil's cave overlooked the ancient town of Cumae, which lies between the two cities.

"That's why I came to see you," said Tarquin. "What is the price for six?"

The Sibyl said, "The same price." Again the king shook his head, so she picked up three more books and tossed them into the flames as well. "These visions too are now lost," she told him.

. The king was horrified by the destruction. Was she mad? Would she burn all these precious books? He ordered his servant to bring his purse and he emptied it on the cave floor, paying the sum that, at the beginning, would have bought him all nine volumes. With a shrug the Sibyl gave him her last three books. Carefully the king carried them back to Rome, where he ordered them housed in a splendid building, to be consulted by the Senate on Rome's most momentous occasions.

In our own times, we too have stories about the power of books. Sometimes they are about the struggle to learn to read; sometimes they are about defying people who want to prevent others from reading.

Another tale is of the sorcerer's apprentice – there's a version of it in the movie *Fantasia* (Mickey Mouse plays the apprentice). It tells of a junior wizard who works hard carrying buckets of water for his magician master. The master won't let his apprentice see his book of spells. He tells the student to concentrate on his chores. One day, the magician goes away. Of course, the student goes straight to the forbidden book. He finds a spell to enchant a broom so that it will bring a bucket of water for him. When that works, the happy apprentice reads more spells and creates many brooms, all carrying pails of water. But the brooms won't stop bringing water, and soon the apprentice realizes that he is going to drown in the magic pouring out of the book. He is only saved when the magician comes back, casts a new spell, and slams the book shut.

There are stories about the power of magical texts in the Bible's Book of Revelation, in Shakespeare's play *The Tempest*, in *The Arabian Nights*, in J.R.R. Tolkien's *The Lord of the Rings*, and in J.K. Rowling's Harry Potter stories. In C.S. Lewis's *The Voyage of the Dawn Treader*, a girl named Lucy opens a magician's book because she wants to help her friends escape his spells, and she finds enchantments both dangerous and wonderful.

What do all these stories have in common?

The ancient idea that writing contains power, and that reading unlocks that power.

This book you are looking at right now is a history of reading. But it is also about people who have been denied the power of reading. It's about lost writing, forbidden books, mistranslations, codes, and vanished libraries. It's about censors, vandals, and spies. It's about people who write in secret. And it's about people who devote their hearts and brains to learning what has been written.

The First Readers

IN ANCIENT TIMES, *the precious skill of reading was reserved for rulers and priests only. But the secret wasn't always theirs to keep.*

In summer in the Mesopotamian plain – what we now call Iraq – the sun beats down like a drum. More than four thousand years ago, it beat down on one of the world's first great cities, Ur, not far from where Baghdad is today. It shone on Ur's people, tens of thousands of them, all the subjects of King Sargon. As they groaned and sweated through the labor of the day, they surely found the heat unbearable. But they left no words of complaint – because they didn't have the skills to put their thoughts into writing. There were people in Ur who could do that, however. Looking down on these workers from the temple walls and palace towers were scribes and priests and priestesses who, for the first time in human history, could read and write.

People had been making marks to keep track of what they produced, owned, and traded even before the time of Ur. Over centuries, these marks grew more complex: drawings of wine jugs and swords, sheep and slaves. But it was in Mesopotamia, around 4,300 years ago, that a few priests, merchants, and royal servants started to simplify picture drawings into something like an alphabet. And it was in Mesopotamia that these readers and writers created some of the world's first works of literature – poems and epic stories such as the *Epic of Gilgamesh*, and the Bible's story of Genesis: how Abraham left his home in Ur for the land of Canaan. Among the earliest of works from Ur are hymns written in honor of Inana, goddess of love and war.

Imagine Ur in those days. The city streets are like an oven, but it's cooler in the shade of the Giparu, a complex of temples and the official home of the En, or high priestess. Inside the Giparu, with her head bowed and her eyes cast down, a servant girl silently pads across the floor in her bare feet to wait on En-hedu-anna (En = high priestess, hedu = ornament, and anna = of the Sky God).

This four-thousand-year-old stone disk shows En-hedu-anna in her pleated robes, flanked by servants. It was discovered during excavations at Ur by a British-American team in 1925–26. "En-hedu-anna" was the great lady's title; we do not know her birth name.

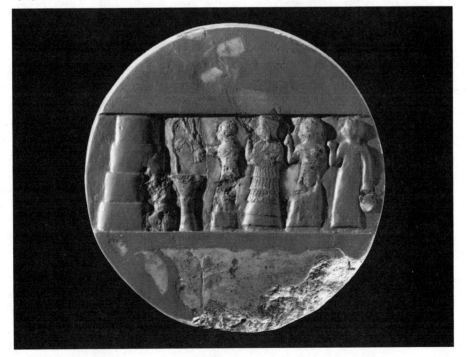

En-hedu-anna – daughter of mighty King Sargon I, conqueror of Ur – pays no attention to mere servants. In carvings from that time, she looks intimidating. She's middle-aged and heavyset, and magnificent in her pleated linen robe. She has huge eyes, lined with age, rimmed in black.

En-hedu-anna's eyes glitter at the approach of a bald scribe, a temple writer, who bows and prostrates himself at En-hedu-anna's feet. The priestess greets him by raising her arm across her face, a gesture known as "letting the hand be at the nose."

Then the two, scribe and priestess, get down to the strange process of writing, while the servant girl quietly watches. The girl knows what writing is; it's the marks priests refer to when they say with great authority, "As it is written. . . ." Writing is the marks that royal messengers consult when they bring word from the king: "Say unto So-and-so," the marks command, and the messenger speaks.

When the ordinary people of Ur – like the girl – pass walls and temples inscribed with writing, they're awe-struck. They can't make writing themselves, but they know that it has power over their lives (some modern people feel this way about computers). Out of more than ten thousand people in Ur, perhaps only a few hundred can actually look at these marks and say the words they represent. But everyone knows that the marks are heavy with knowledge, and that they can carry knowledge from one person to another, or from the past into tomorrow.

The scribe shows the high priestess a clay tablet small enough to sit on the palm of his brown hand. En-hedu-anna studies it. It is lined with writing marks, like the tracks of small birds, in row on orderly row.

High Priestess En-hedu-anna reads aloud from the tablet. It is a poem she composed when her father's enemy, a king of Uruk, rebelled against King Sargon. "Let silence fall onto the rebel land. . . . Until it submits, let spit be poured on it!" Her poem, ferocious and exultant, tells of how rebels are crushed when the goddess of war herself appears, "joyfully beautiful, armed with the seven maces!"

En-hedu-anna dictates the ending of her latest poem to the scribe, who records the words by pressing a stylus (stick of wood) with a sharpened tip into the clay's soft, wet surface. The resulting marks look like wedges with long tails, which is why archeologists call this writing *cuneiform*, or wedge-writing. *Cuneus* is Latin for "wedge." Then En-hedu-anna commands the scribe to pass the stylus to her, and she adds something, firmly pressing the stylus into the clay. "There, it is finished," she declares. The scribe studies what she has written and reverently reads it out loud: "The compiler of these tablets was En-hedu-anna. My king, something has been created that no one has created before." (Nowadays, some scholars at the University of Pennsylvania Museum say En-hedu-anna was right to claim that she had created something new. As far as we know, the high priestess was the first person in history to write a poem – and to sign her name to it.)

The servant girl looks away. She is hiding a terrible, wonderful secret. She has seen the marks for En-hedu-anna's name so many times that she can pick those special cuneiform characters out from the rest. She well knows that lowly servants like herself are not supposed to understand the sacred mysteries of reading. But she can read an author's name. She has pressed open the door, just a little.

2

Language Lost and Language Found

SOME OF THE ancient world's greatest cultures had the skill of reading and then lost it. The history of reading is full of dead ends, forgotten voices, and mysteries.

Little Arthur Evans, small for his seven years of age but very strong, looked proudly at the deep hole he had dug all by himself in the garden of the Evans family home – Nash Mills, in Hertfordshire, in England. No one had seen him dig – except perhaps the ghost of his dear mother, who had died the year before, in 1857. From a piece of special fabric Arthur unwrapped an old doll, and laid it in the hole in the ground. Delicately he placed a dead butterfly on top. Then he unfolded a piece of paper on which he had printed KING EDWARD SIXTH AND THE BUTTERFLY AND THEIR CLOTHS AND THINGS. He gently covered his diggings with earth.

Not long after, Arthur's father – John Evans, a wealthy paper manufacturer – was walking by the garden and noticed the toy grave. He removed the earth, examined Arthur's note, and later wrote to one of his friends about his son's strange passion for digging and making up stories about what was buried there: "He is a very odd child."

John Evans also liked digging. He was an amateur geologist and anthropologist. (Geologists study rocks and the structure of our planet; anthropologists unearth the structure of human societies.) Sometimes he took Arthur on his expeditions. Often, he invited scientists over for dinner parties and discussions of the latest findings of fossils, bones, and ancient tools. When little Arthur wasn't hanging around listening to the grown-ups talk about Roman pottery or buried weapons, he read. He particularly liked books such as Charles Kingsley's *The Heroes*, which retold ancient Greek myths – including the story of Theseus.

All his long life, Arthur would think about this tale: how Theseus, a brave prince, sailed from Greece to the island of Crete to fight the Minotaur, a monster with a bull's head who lived in a labyrinth, or maze. The monster's master, King Minos of Crete, was very cruel. He used to send strangers into the labyrinth, knowing that they would get lost in its twisting passages, and that his Minotaur would leap out of the shadows and kill them. But the king's daughter, Ariadne, fell in love with Theseus and didn't want him to die. She gave him a long thread so that he could find his way through the labyrinth and slay the Minotaur.

This story haunted Arthur. So did other Greek myths that he read when he went off to boarding school. In the 1800s, most European schoolboys studied the Greek poet Homer's story of the Trojan War – of how in ancient times Greek warriors besieged the city of Troy, but could not get inside its walls. At last, the cunning Odysseus told his fellow Greeks to build a giant, hollow wooden horse and leave it on the beach. The Trojans thought the horse was a gift, so they opened their gates and dragged it inside the city walls. At night, some Greeks hiding inside climbed out of the hollow horse, opened the city gates to their companions, and burned mighty Troy to the ground.

Arthur Evans's teachers told him that the tale of Theseus, and Homer's story of the fall of Troy, were myths, important mostly because they inspired real people. When Alexander the Great had set out to conquer the world, he had carried copies of Homer's two great heroic poems, the *Iliad* (about the Trojan War) and the *Odyssey* (about the travels of Odysseus). But Alexander was fact and the Trojan War was fiction, insisted the scholars. In a twelve-volume history of Greece published in England in 1856 – when Arthur was five – one British expert had written of the Trojan War, "It is, in the eyes of modern inquiry, essentially a legend and nothing more."

Then one June morning in 1871, Arthur, not yet twenty years old, snapped open his newspaper and read that an eccentric German millionaire, Heinrich Schliemann, was claiming he'd found the real, historical city of Troy.

Schliemann was self-educated, neither a scholar nor historian, and no one could convince him that Homer had written this great poem about something that had never happened. Because Homer had written that Troy was built on a windy plain near the coast of the "wine-dark sea," Schliemann looked for such a place, and started digging up a rubble-covered mound in northwest Turkey called Hissarlik. Within days, Schliemann, his young Greek wife, Sophia, and their team of diggers had unearthed huge stone walls. And then more walls, and more. They'd found not just Troy but many Troys – destroyed, rebuilt, destroyed again. Signs of fire, signs of war. Ancient cities in layers, each built on the ruins of the last. Homer's Troy, the Schliemanns announced, was the ruin that dated from twelve hundred years before the time of Christ.

The world was thunderstruck.

Heroes of modern archeology, the Schliemanns moved on to Mycenae, in Greece, and dug up what they said was the city of King Agamemnon, who had led the Greeks in the Trojan War. In 1877, the Schliemanns exhibited their Trojan and Mycenaean treasures – necklaces, earrings, headdresses – in London. People lined up for hours to see them.

Arthur was among them. What he saw only made him wonder more about these long-ago civilizations. The jewelry and pottery shards and weapons on display made it clear that Mycenae and Troy had been

Sir Arthur Evans with the walking stick he called Prodger, in the Palace of Minos, Crete, in 1922. It must have been winter, Crete's rainy season; almost no rain falls on the island in the broiling hot summer months.

sophisticated cultures of laws and learning. But where was the writing? Where were the tablets or scrolls written at the time of Troy's great wars? Why couldn't we learn about these events from the people who lived through them?

Arthur Evans made this question the challenge of his life. In 1883, on a trip to Greece, he dropped in on the Schliemanns in Athens. The famous German told his young English visitor that archeology's next great challenge would be to find the palace of King Minos in Crete. Alas, it was too dangerous to go there, because of a savage civil war. Even so, after Schliemann died in 1890, Arthur Evans and his father decided to spend the family fortune to see if more Greek legends were true. The Schliemanns had already proved that Homer's stories were based on history. Arthur Evans wanted to see that history in writing.

Don't bother, the experts told him. They said that when the Trojan War had occurred, around 1200 BCE, no one in Europe had been able to read or write. Yes, a few people around Ur had been literate, and there was evidence of writing among the ancient Chinese and Egyptians. But the Jews hadn't written anything down until around 800 BCE. Why would the Greeks have been any faster? Besides, the scholars agreed, Homer had lived some five hundred years after the Trojan War, and his poems had been composed for oral performance – to be recited for people who could not read. Like songs, oral poetry repeats a lot of phrases over and over to help the reciters remember, and to help the listeners follow. Homer had his formulas, like "cunning Odysseus" or "wine-dark sea," because his listeners weren't able to go leafing back through a book to remind themselves of who someone was, or what had happened earlier in the story. They had no books, and surely their ancestors half a millennium earlier had had none.

The experts' arguments didn't stop Arthur Evans. He was stubbornly convinced that whoever had made the treasures of Mycenae and Troy must have been able to read and write. When he'd visited Athens' antique shops, he'd bought stones engraved with odd marks – lettering that wasn't Greek, or Egyptian, or the language of Ur, for that matter. No one knew what civilization the writing came from. But some of these stones had come from the island of Crete. So Arthur Evans went to Crete and, like Schliemann, he let Homer be his guide.

Homer had written that in Crete was "a countless multitude of men and ninety cities. Among these is the great city of Knossos." If one wanted to find samples of Crete's ancient writing, surely they would be in the island's greatest city. But where was Knossos?

A Greek archeologist, Minos Kalokairinos, told the Englishman that he had a strong suspicion about a wild, overgrown mound called Kephala. The Greek had dug a little there himself, but he didn't have the money to buy the land or hire a team. The rich Englishman did.

On March 23, 1900, Arthur Evans's team of Cretan laborers set their shovels into Kephala. Within two days they unearthed the remains of a palace. As its walls were exposed to the brilliant sunshine, the diggers could see fragments of wall paintings. Later, the fragments were pieced together to reveal bronze-skinned athletes leaping over bulls (shades of the Minotaur!), and beautiful women with black curls (as lovely as Princess Ariadne!).

Excitedly waving the walking stick he always carried (he called it Prodger), Arthur paced the emerging ruins. After only a few more days, the workmen began finding clay tablets covered with strange marks. They looked like the marks on those stones in the Athens antique stores. People long ago had written on the clay when it was damp enough to press in a mark, and then let it harden. But while most clay tablets didn't last long, these ones did, because a dreadful fire in the palace had baked them rock-solid.

Arthur had no idea what language he was looking at. The symbols looked like mugs and bow ties and forks. Anyone who could read this language had been dead for over three thousand years. Waving Prodger, he urged his diggers to bring him more samples. Meanwhile, he sent word back to London that he had found King Minos's palace at Knossos, and that he'd found writing from the long-lost civilization as well. The news flashed round the world. A reporter at *The New York Times* got so carried away with enthusiasm that he wrote, "Are we to catch a glimpse of a Homeric god as he lived in the flesh?"

In Greek myths, the gods like to tease mere mortals. Perhaps they were teasing Arthur Evans. He was knighted in 1911, and built a grand house near the diggings and named it the Villa Ariadne, after King Minos's daughter. For thirty years, he and his team sweated and slaved under the blazing blue Cretan sky. More wall paintings, treasures, and tablets emerged from Kephala's soil. Yet Sir Arthur could never decode the tablets.

The best he could do was identify three different kinds of writing. The oldest, from the deepest layers of the digging, seemed to be a kind of picture-writing. Then came what he called Linear A – part picture, part alphabet. The writing from the upper layers he called Linear B.

Linear B consisted of about ninety unfamiliar characters. That number was important; picture-based systems of writing, like Chinese, have

Michael Ventris (shown here in the early 1950s) made the first breakthrough in decoding Linear B, but he turned for help to John Chadwick, a specialist in ancient Greek who had worked as a military code-breaker during World War II.

thousands of characters. The closer you get to an alphabet-based system of writing, using letters like blocks to build the sounds of words, the fewer characters you need (our alphabet has twenty-six letters; the modern Greek alphabet has only twenty-four letters). So Sir Arthur figured that with ninety marks, Linear B was probably in between a picture system and an alphabet-based system – some sort of syllable system, where the characters didn't stand for single letters but for sounds (a little like license-plate code: I C U, Q T!).

The problem is that you can only figure out a code if you know what language it is written in. Because Sir Arthur had discovered Minoan civilization, he insisted that "his" Minoans were utterly unique, and had dominated their ancient world. When other scholars dared to suggest that the people of Knossos might have spoken ancient Greek, he used his considerable influence to have them shut up and shut out of scholarly conferences. He insisted that everyone from the time of King Minos had spoken Minoan – whatever that was.

Now another person comes into the story. In 1936, a fourteen-year-old schoolboy named Michael Ventris went to one of Sir Arthur's lectures, and he heard the great man admit again that he could not read Linear B. After the lecture, Michael was introduced to Sir Arthur, who was leaning heavily on his stick, Prodger, for support. Sir Arthur's accomplishments, and his frustration, left Michael feeling impressed.

Then war came, and distracted the world from the mysteries of lost languages. In April 1941, Greece fell to the Nazis. The Greek royal family fled to Crete, and hid at Sir Arthur's Villa Ariadne. By the end of May they fled again – because the Nazis stormed ashore and made the Villa Ariadne their headquarters. The Nazis shot Greek and English archeologists. Back in England, old Sir Arthur heard about the bloodshed, and was heartsick. He died on July 11, 1941.

But after his death, archeologists were free to try out new ideas. Legions of them, inspired by visions of the heroic times of Theseus and Troy, turned their brains to the job of decoding the lost language of Crete.

Some tried comparing Linear B to other unusual languages – Basque (from a region in Spain) and even Finnish. None had any luck. One – Alice Kober, who taught classical Greek at Brooklyn College in New York – got closer than all the others, by using a code-breaker strategy from the world of military intelligence. She assigned each of the Linear B characters a number, and marked down which combinations of numbers occurred most frequently. Then she published charts showing the most common combinations of syllables.

Five years after the war ended, the now grown-up Michael Ventris studied Alice Kober's work and, excited, wrote her a letter. She was dying of lung cancer, and never wrote back, so Ventris plowed on alone. What if the most frequent combinations on the Kober charts were the names of places? He tried out a hunch that 70-52-12 might be Ko-no-so . . . Knossos?

Using place names as a key, Ventris assigned sounds to other numbers. Things clicked into place. Sir Arthur Evans had been wrong; Linear B seemed to be some early form of Greek. Working with John Chadwick, a Cambridge University professor, Michael Ventris announced in June 1953 that Linear B could finally be read once more. (Alas, Linear A remains a mystery to this day.)

But what a shock for the romantically inspired archeologists who had devoted their lives to rediscovering the world of Homer's tales! Deciphered, the Linear B tablets turned out to be official records of chariot repairs, grain-storage orders, and cloth shipments. The writing revealed a lost civilization, not of godlike heroes, but of bureaucrats and customs agents.

And war. The state in which the tablets were found – baked by catastrophic fires – confirmed that whatever civilization flourished at Knossos had been destroyed by invaders around 1300 BCE. The historians gradually pieced together what had happened, and it was a reminder that reading is a precious skill that can always be lost. The invasions of Knossos by people from the mainland had crushed the civilization of the elegant, stylish people who wrote in Linear B. A Dark Age had followed, a time of violence and destruction. People on Crete and in mainland Greece had slipped backwards into illiteracy and ignorance. Struggling to survive, they had forgotten how to paint on walls, make complex weapons, or write things down. They had forgotten a lot – except for their stories, which were passed down through the generations by poets like Homer. Finally, around 700 BCE – just after the time of Homer – they adopted a brand-new alphabet from the Phoenicians, who lived west of Ur, and started all over again to learn reading and writing.

Today, thanks to people such as Heinrich Schliemann and Arthur Evans, we have proof that Troy and Knossos existed. But after all the archeologists' digging, we still don't know if the heroes of Homer (or whoever composed the *Iliad* and the *Odyssey*) knew any alphabet at all. There are passages in Homer where the warriors sing heroic songs. There are none in which they can read.

The Poet and the Emperor

WRITERS OFTEN HOPE that what they set down will change the ideas of other people and of future generations. But these world-changing ambitions can put writers themselves into deadly danger.

Marcus Annaeus Lucan ordered his slaves to carry his litter into the jostling crowds of the city of Rome. The crowds stank of sweat and fried food. You could smell the raw sewage. Yet Lucan was very pleased to be back at the center of the Roman Empire, after his years of study in Greece. In AD 60, rich young Romans often went to Greece to round out their education – in fact, the Romans respected Greek civilization so much that they claimed Rome had been founded by a Trojan prince who'd fled after the Trojan War. But Greece's days of glory were dimming, and by the first century after the time of Christ, Rome, with a population of more than a million people, was one of the greatest cities in the world.

Held aloft by his slaves, Lucan moved happily through the city's teeming streets, ignoring the foreigners from all over the empire who babbled in exotic languages, the cries from merchants selling furs from Germania, wool from Britannia, and spices from Africa and Asia.

This colossal marble head of Nero Claudius Caesar was carved a year or two after the emperor murdered his mother. His expression looks haunted; Nero used to complain that ghosts followed him around with whips and flaming torches.

At last his litter came to an entire street devoted to the publishing industry. Scribes copied out manuscripts here, and merchants shipped the scrolls to the far corners of the empire. The shops also sold a new kind of book called a codex – square, with pages that turned instead of unrolling (the Roman emperor Julius Caesar had found these books more convenient than scrolls when he was a military commander fighting on the battlefield).

Lucan was pleased to see that the publishing business was booming. For the first time in human history, the booksellers boasted, it was possible to be an international bestselling author. This claim interested Lucan deeply. He was not just an ordinary rich young man. He was a poet – a poet living at the center of an empire ruled by someone who might just prove to be one of the greatest champions of writers the world had yet seen: Emperor Nero Claudius Drusus Caesar.

Of course, Emperor Nero was crazy. A strange-looking redhead, Nero liked to think of himself as a talented singer and actor. This scandalized Rome – an emperor was supposed to be worshiped as a god, yet Nero would go before an audience to play the part of a woman, or a slave! But that wasn't the biggest scandal. Nero came from a bad family – the family of Julius Caesar, who had destroyed the Roman republic more than a century before, in a civil war. Ever since Julius Caesar had made himself the first emperor, Rome's politics had been dominated by ruthless men. Nero's uncle, the insane Emperor Caligula, had murdered many people (including his own pregnant sister), and had been so jealous of Homer, for being more famous than Caligula, that he had ordered Homer's books to be burned in public.

And all Rome had heard the story that Nero's mother, Agrippina, had once been told by an astrologer, "You will give birth to a son who will be emperor but who will kill you." At which the ambitious Agrippina had shrugged. "*Necet me dum regnet,*" she had said. ("Let him kill me, so long as he rules.") Sure enough, the year before Lucan's return from Greece, in AD 59, Nero had tried to kill his mother – not once but three times.

Even so, it seemed like a good time for a young writer like Lucan to capture the public's attention. The usual way to do that was by giving public readings in auditoriums, or in open-air theaters. Over in Greece, people used to sit in theaters listening to Homer's *Iliad* and *Odyssey* told aloud by special reciters known as rhapsodes (our word "rhapsody" comes from this) who could recite all sixteen thousand lines from memory. By Lucan's time, upper-class Greeks and Romans had their own private libraries, but public performances were still the test of a good poet. And Emperor Nero loved public readings. Lucan decided it would be good for his career to arrange to read before the emperor. He asked his uncle, who just happened to be Seneca, Nero's private adviser, for an introduction.

Lucan and Uncle Seneca no doubt discussed whether it was a wise idea to get close to a man as crazy as Nero. They surely discussed the rumors about Nero's mother, too. All Rome knew that Agrippina had been blocking

Nero's plans to ditch his wife and marry his girlfriend. The emperor had told his meddling mother to take a cruise in the Bay of Naples, where he arranged to have a ship's mast fall and crush her. But it missed. So the sailors threw Agrippina overboard. The emperor's mother swam ashore! Finally, someone stabbed her – someone in Nero's pay. In any case, she was gone.

And yet it seemed that she wasn't gone. After Agrippina's death, the emperor started seeing ghosts. Old Seneca advised Nero to seek comfort in books, and the company of writers such as his amusing nephew Lucan. But be careful, said Seneca to Lucan. Don't get too close.

Lucan was sure he could handle the situation. The two men were introduced. The emperor decided that he liked Lucan, who was just two years younger than he was. Best of all, he liked Lucan's poetry. Nero made his new best friend a Roman senator at age twenty-four, the youngest senator in Rome's history. Soon, the two young men were carousing around the city in true imperial style, stuffing themselves on larks and pigs and figs and cheese and wine at noisy banquets, and then staggering down to the room known as the vomitorium to empty themselves so they could enjoy yet more food and drink. Late into the night they carried on, roaring out poems and complimenting each other on their talent, and planning the city's biggest public spectacle ever: the first Neronian Games, modeled on the Olympics, with chariot races, gladiators, acrobats, and poets – starring themselves, of course.

The Neronian Games were duly held. Lucan dazzled the audiences with a sort of rap performance – a made-up-on-the-spot poem about the Greek legend of Orpheus. What earned him first prize, however, was his poem "Laudes Neroni," which means "In Praise of Nero." Soldiers were stationed throughout the crowds to encourage cheering. Audience members who didn't cheer soon got the message. The Neronian Games were a huge success.

But when the cheering stopped, the emperor's bad dreams returned. And now Nero had a new nightmare: What if the Romans thought Lucan was a better poet than he was?

Meanwhile, Lucan was pleased by the attention his public readings were getting, the way his words could move a crowd to excitement and tears. Perhaps he had fallen in love with the idea that he could use his poetry for a good cause, such as saving Rome. If so, he wouldn't have been the first or last poet to believe that his words had the power to change the world.

Lucan began to write an epic poem that would show how things had started to go wrong for Rome with Julius Caesar's civil war. Late in the year 63, he announced that he would give a public reading. Invitations went out, seating was assembled in the auditorium, wine was poured, torches were lit. Scores of people turned up, maybe hundreds, for Lucan was a star. The emperor himself swept in, his bulgy blue eyes watching Lucan closely. Nero's presence was an honor. The audience murmured in excitement.

As Lucan began to recite his *Bellum Civile* (*The Civil War*), a rhapsody of blood and heroism, his listeners noted that Nero seemed to enjoy the opening sequences. The emperor especially liked the lines about the civil war being worth all the suffering because it would ultimately bring Nero to power. Everyone cheered Lucan's stirring descriptions of Julius Caesar smiting the Belgians and the long-haired Gauls.

After a time, however, the audience began to stir uneasily in their chairs and to sneak glances at the emperor. For by now Lucan's story was about Romans fighting Romans. In one particularly gory sequence, Lucan described a Roman naval leader who chose to die rather than surrender to Julius Caesar. The audience could scarcely believe it; Lucan was making Caesar sound like a power-hungry villain.

Nero's smile grew cold and thin. This foolish poet was insulting the emperor's own ancestor. As the Roman historian Suetonius tells it, Nero may have attended the event just to give Lucan the Big Freeze (Suetonius actually uses the word *refrigerandi*). Nero suddenly stood up and strode from the auditorium, his guards following. If he thought Lucan would take the hint, he was mistaken.

The summer of 64 was hot and dry. One July night, fire broke out in the oldest quarter of the city. Fanned by summer winds, it swept through Rome for six days. Though Nero personally helped to fight the flames, the story spread that the crazy emperor had purposely set the fire just so he could redesign the city. The Romans also whispered that Nero had fiddled – played music, that is – while Rome burned. The emperor blamed the fire on the Christians (he hated them, in any case, for denying his godliness), and put a few hundred to death. It was no use; ordinary Romans were starting to turn against him.

The wild partying and the Romans' growing hatred of Nero were making Lucan and Seneca think hard about the good old days of the Roman republic, when the people had elected senators who ruled wisely. They weren't the only ones thinking such treasonous thoughts. Many longed for better government than Rome was getting from its lunatic emperor.

After Lucan performed another offensive public reading, this one about the fire, Nero issued a decree forbidding him to give any more such readings. The punishment was mild compared to the tortures the emperor routinely ordered for the Christians. But this was in the time before printing presses, when readings were the best way to reach the public. Lucan was being censored, shut down. As a popular poet admired throughout Rome for his performances, he was finished.

Lucan shrugged when he heard the sentence. In his elegant villa, he kept on writing. His work-in-progress, *Bellum Civile*, was becoming more openly critical of Nero. He didn't seem to care if it was treasonous; he was swept along by the power of the story he was telling. When he went out, according to Suetonius, people overheard him making jokes about the emperor in public baths and public toilets, the places where Romans met to gossip. It got so bad that Lucan was scaring the other customers.

Word of Lucan's break with Nero reached the ears of certain men plotting to overthrow the emperor and bring back more honest rule. One winter day early in AD 65, the plotters invited Lucan to join their conspiracy to kill Nero. Lucan agreed.

This was a deadly mistake. Nero's spies overheard one of the plotters, an educated slave girl named Epicharis, and arrested her. When the other rebels learned that she was in prison, they sped up their plans. They decided to tackle Nero at the public games, trip him, and drive in the knife. Alas, the group tripped themselves when one conspirator, a melodramatic man named Scevinus, couldn't resist making a big speech to his household slaves, explaining that he was about to attempt a heroic deed that might cost him his life. The slaves figured out what their boss was talking about. To save their own skins, they told the emperor's guards. Nero ordered everyone rounded up, including old Seneca.

Epicharis, questioned under torture, refused to reveal anything. The Roman aristocrats weren't as brave as the slave girl. Once in custody, they quickly started ratting on each other, hoping it would win them mercy. It didn't. Seneca, Scevinus, Lucan, and the other plotters were sentenced to die.

On April 30, AD 65, the emperor's guards pounded on the door of Lucan's villa, and announced that the time had come for him to commit suicide. Because he had once been Nero's friend, he could do it any way he chose.

Lucan's family called in a surgeon to help make the death more comfortable. Sitting in a warm bath, surrounded by his wife, servants, family, and friends, Lucan ordered a servant to bring him the last scroll from his unfinished poem. According to the historian Tacitus, Lucan died reciting a passage about a wounded warrior facing his end on the battlefield. He died reading his forbidden masterpiece.

Lucan's words had led him into trouble – but at the very end, they gave him strength. As for Nero, the Roman people rose up against him just three years after Lucan's death. The singing emperor had to kill himself to avoid being executed. His last words were "*Qualis artifex pereo!*" ("What an artist perishes!")

Two thousand years later, university libraries still stock Lucan's poetry. You can still read *Bellum Civile*. But you can't read Nero's poems. Nobody seems to have thought they were worth preserving.

The Made-to-Order Alphabet

SOME LANGUAGES INCLUDE such distinctive sounds that they cannot be expressed in other people's alphabets. If the people who speak these languages want to read their own stories, they have to find their own ways of writing them.

Dismay flickers across the faces of the courtiers and warriors in the court of Vramshapouh, King of the Armenians. Reports are coming back to the royal city of Vagarshabad (near the modern capital, Yerevan), from monks across the land, that Armenia's children will not, or cannot, learn to read.

Armenia, east of Troy and north of Ur, is a land of blast-furnace plains and wild mountains. It is so hot around salty Lake Van (in ancient Armenia but in modern Turkey) that the local cats have learned to swim. It grows cooler in the orchards of apricots and almonds that lead toward the jagged, snowy mountains. The biggest is Ararat, where Noah's Ark is said to have landed after the Great Flood. Part of the Roman Empire since the time of Julius Caesar, Armenia has a proudly independent spirit and was the first nation in the world to adopt Christianity, in the year AD 301. (The Roman Empire, under attack by barbarians, did so a generation later.)

But by the year 400, King Vramshapouh fears for his country. Some of its people still follow "the diabolical worship of demons," writes a monk of that time, Gorioun. Meanwhile, church leaders in the Roman Empire's new eastern capital, Constantinople (modern-day Istanbul), keep interfering with Armenia's churches, trying to appoint bishops and generally take charge. Constantinople cannot be trusted; its rulers keep cutting deals with the Persians – the enemies on Armenia's eastern side – to carve up Armenia between them. Armenians can only trust themselves. And King Vramshapouh, looking at the fiercest warriors in his court, knows that his country cannot survive by the power of the sword alone. He needs God on his side, and he needs his people to follow the same God.

The king and his monks decide that, to unify the country, they must teach all Armenians to read the Christian Gospels. A Syrian bishop named Daniel sends an alphabet to Vagarshabad, and King Vramshapouh orders that it be taught to his country's young people. But now, two years later, monks are bringing back reports that this alphabet is unteachable.

The king stares at the ranks of burning-eyed, bearded Christians who have worked with him on his national dream. At length the monk Mesrob Mashtots steps forward to speak, and the king settles back in relief, listening closely. In fact everyone in the court listens, because Mesrob used to be a military adviser before he became a soldier of God. He has studied at great centers of the early Christian Church, and has learned to read and write all the languages of early Christian texts – Aramaic, Greek, and Syriac.

Mesrob tells the court why the alphabet sent by the Syrian bishop is unteachable. It's too much like Syriac and Hebrew; it has hardly any vowels. (Anyone who has studied Hebrew for a bar mitzvah or bat mitzvah knows how hard it is to read an alphabet without vowels. It's like trying to guess whether CT stands for CAT or COT or CUT or CUTE or COOT.) Because Armenian is a language rich in complex vowel sounds, an alphabet without vowels cannot express enough distinctions. Mesrob says Armenia must find a new alphabet, to teach its children in its own way.

To purify his spirit and transform himself from a soldier into a man of God, Mesrob Mashtots is said to have endured great hardship: hunger, thirst, cold, sleeping in caves, and eating only herbs.

Mesrob bows to the king, his long black beard bobbing almost to his knees, and announces that he will personally take up the challenge. With the king's permission, he will depart immediately for the city of Edessa, on the border between Persia and the Christian world, to study the best alphabets of East and West.

This is a bold plan. Edessa in AD 400 is on the frontier of faiths. It is abuzz with heresies and strange ideas, and home to devil worshippers, moon worshippers, magicians, Persian Zoroastrians, Hindus from India. There are Christian sects that follow the Jewish Laws of Moses, Indian-influenced Christians who believe that Christ keeps coming back through reincarnation, and even Marcionite Christians, who worship the Serpent from the Garden of Eden. Edessa is also haunted by remnants of pagan religions from the time of Ur. The place is famous for its holy fishponds, where huge carp, said to have been sacred to an ancient Mesopotamian goddess of war and love, churn through muddy brown waters.

Into this murmuring marketplace of ideas strides Mesrob, robe and beard flying, followed by his most loyal monks. Like a general, he orders his men to fan out across the city and spend their days collecting a scroll here, a codex there, and consulting all the scholars they can find. The Armenians visit Greek scholars, who speak and write the tongue of Homer. They find men of the south who use the cursive Aramaic alphabet (the language of Jesus). They talk with travelers from the western reaches of the dying Roman Empire, where the Roman alphabet (our own) has been chiseled into stone monuments from Caledonia (Scotland) to Pannonia (Hungary).

Meanwhile, Mesrob prays for guidance. Every day, according to his biographer, Gorioun, he takes pieces of parchment and tries out "all the variations of letters, thin and heavy strokes, long and short, single letters as well as combinations. . . ." He works in every alphabet he can, searching for the one that most easily expresses, in the Armenian tongue, the opening passage of the Bible's Proverbs of Solomon: "To know wisdom and instruction, to perceive the words of understanding. . . ."

And then, according to ancient Armenian writings, "there appeared in his heart before his mind's eye a right hand writing upon stone . . . and all the details of all the letters accumulated in his mind as if on a plate. . . ." Some people later call this vision a miracle from God. Whatever it is, Mesrob summons his fellow soldiers of literacy and announces a victory. They have an alphabet – not some foreign hand-me-down, but a brand-new one inspired just for them.

He shows them his vision. Mesrob's alphabet has thirty-six characters compared to our twenty-six. Twenty letters seem to have grown out of Greek, eight seem similar to Persian, and one or two are like Syriac. The letters are detached, rather than flowing together as they do in Syriac. As in Greek, Mesrob tells his fellow monks, the letters are to be read from left to right. The monks see at once that this alphabet is complex enough to express the sounds of their own language. With the announcement of Mesrob's miracle, "There arose from all the churches hymns of praise," writes the monk Gorioun, "praise glorifying God. . . ."

At last Mesrob and his band of monks can turn their backs on Edessa's snake worshippers and sacred fishponds. They begin their long walk home to the land of Mount Ararat. As they near Vagarshabad, says Gorioun, "The assembled courtiers of King Vramshapouh came in a throng outside the royal city to meet them . . . singing hymns and doxologies. . . ."

This is the Armenian alphabet of Mesrob's time, with thirty-six letters. In the Middle Ages, as the language evolved, extra letters were added and the shape of the letters became more rounded.

Mesrob's alphabet is shown to teachers, who instruct the children. The children learn to read. They grow up to teach their own children to read Armenian, generation after generation.

Armenian monks showed their writing system to monks from Georgia and Ethiopia; while modern scholars of alphabets believe the Georgian and Ethiopian alphabets developed on their own, there's a legend that Mesrob helped these monks write the Gospels in their own tongue.

Sixteen hundred years after the time of Mesrob, a young Canadian artist was hiking in the Blue Mountains region of central Jamaica, and he walked into a village of Rastafarians (Jamaicans with religious roots in Ethiopia). Several tall, stern Rastamen with dreadlocks gathered round. Their leader asked the Canadian's name, and the Canadian told him.

"Is that an Armenian name?" the Rastafarian asked.

"Er, yes," said the baffled artist, nervously.

"Then," said the Rastaman, with a big smile, "you are welcome here. We are all children of Mesrob."

The Prayerful Pagodas

STRANGE AS IT sounds, some of the earliest printed texts were never meant to be read by human beings. Simply publishing them seemed to be enough to conjure up reading's divine power.

The magnificence of buildings such as the Kasuga Shrine at Nara, capital of Japan at the time of the Buddhist Empress Shotoku, alienated ordinary people who lived in simple huts and were loyal to an older religion.

ara is an ancient city of deer parks, and massive wooden temples with red lacquer pillars. Somewhere deep inside the Imperial Palace, late at night, Empress Shotoku, the ruler of Japan, and her spiritual adviser, the Buddhist monk Dokyo, sit deep in consultation. It is around the year AD 764 by the Western calendar, and the empress is telling Dokyo that they are both in danger. Although a rebellion by Japanese noble families against the growing power of Buddhist monks has just been suppressed and the leader, Fujiwara Nakamaro, has been executed, the rebels are still a threat.

As empress and monk bend their heads together, the scene looks intimate. Maybe it is. Some gossips at the palace say that the empress, who is herself a Buddhist nun, is in love with the monk. Everyone says she spends far too much time in Dokyo's company.

Her Imperial Majesty speaks in a low voice of her fears. Powerful members of the Fujiwara clan, who would do anything to stop Buddhism, have been spreading stories that she is Dokyo's pawn – that Dokyo is using her so he can take over the throne himself.

This accusation makes Dokyo smile quietly. It's true, the empress is very dependent on him. What, she asks him now, can be done to ensure that rebels never again threaten her power?

The monk counsels calm. With great firmness he tells the empress that she must make an impressive gesture that will promote peace in her realm, and assure Japan's Buddhists that she is committed to their faith. She must order a million prayers – *darani*, or Buddhist incantations – to be copied out and sent around her empire. A million prayers.

A million? How can this be done? The empress cannot conceal her concern. There are not enough scribes in the whole kingdom to write fast enough. And the rebels could rise against her again, at any time!

Dokyo is so reassuring, so helpful in her time of fear. He tells her that it is not impossible to produce a million prayers – not if she orders workmen to make use of a miraculous new technique developed in mainland China and Korea. This technique is called printing.

The Empress Shotoku raises one perfect eyebrow.

Here's how it works, Dokyo explains. The prayers must be carved into blocks of wood or cast in metal, with the letters standing off the surface. Then the raised letters will be covered in ink. When pieces of mulberry paper are pressed against the letters – behold! The writing shows up on the paper. Printing, says Dokyo, can produce many copies quickly – thousands, maybe tens of thousands, before the letters wear out.

Let it be done, says the empress.

And so, in the year 764, a Japanese empress launches the biggest publishing operation the world had so far seen. Blocks of wood are carved, bronze molds are cast, paper is inked, and prayers are printed. Workers insert the printed strips of paper through holes in the tops of a million wooden models of pagodas (temples), each about the size of an adult hand. The model pagodas are loaded onto carts that set out across Japan, delivering a hundred thousand pagodas to each of ten carefully chosen sites.

Even with printing technology, the Hyakumanto Darani or "Million-Pagoda Prayers" project takes about six years to complete. The empress's pious gesture only adds to the fears that she is going to give the throne to Dokyo. After Empress Shotoku dies, the Fujiwara family rises up again, and seizes power. The Fujiwaras move the imperial court from Nara to Kyoto and force Dokyo to leave Japan. Then Japan passes a law forbidding women to ever again become rulers.

As the centuries pass, many of the little wooden pagodas disappear, are given away, or are lost to fires and wars. But right up until our own times, a few hundred remain. Inside, their paper prayer strips stay intact – because no one ever reads them.

Empress Shotoku and her monk didn't want the prayers to be read. They only wanted to demonstrate religious duty by causing the words to be copied out a million times. The world's first great publishing effort was about harnessing the power of words to create an effect. Actually letting people read those words had nothing to do with it.

6

The Stolen Story

IN SOME SOCIETIES, certain groups – such as women – weren't supposed to read or write about "important" subjects such as history, philosophy, or economics. A Japanese woman of the Heian period responded by writing one of the world's first bestsellers – a novel.

It is the year AD 1009, and Lady Murasaki Shikibu, normally one of the most composed and dignified ladies in the court of Empress Shoshi of Japan, is frantic. She overturns mats and rummages through chests and boxes in her room in the palace in Kyoto. Where are the papers on which she has written rough drafts of the latest chapters of her novel?

Lady Murasaki sits down suddenly on her heels, and bows her head into the folds of her silk kimono. There can be no doubt about it. Someone must have pushed aside the paper screens, entered her private chamber, and removed her handwritten copy of *Genji Monogatari – The Tale of Genji.* Someone who could not wait to find out what happens next in the Shining Prince's adventures with beautiful highborn women . . . what jealousy, what romance . . . what dark and unexpected corners of the prince's character might be revealed. . . .

Lady Murasaki's novel, The Tale of Genji, *has inspired artists for a thousand years. This woodcut by a Kyoto artist, Yamamoto Shunsho, was first published in 1650.*

Lady Murasaki is outraged. The latest chapters are not ready to be read. They have not been polished, checked for style, or sent to scribes for elegant transcriptions (by this time the Japanese know how to do block printing, but books are still copied out by hand). *Genji* could have been stolen by almost anyone; the story is very popular. In fact, it is the reason Lady Murasaki was invited to court in the first place.

After the death of her husband, the governor of Yamashiro province, around the year 999, Lady Murasaki expected to spend the rest of her life behind the walls of her own house. Highborn women's lives in medieval

Japan are limited; they're allowed to read, but it is thought unladylike if they show interest in "serious" subjects such as philosophy, science, or heroic histories. They are also strongly discouraged from writing using the complex Chinese system, which involves thousands of characters for words and syllables (Lady Murasaki knows how to read and write Chinese-style, but other ladies mock her for being a showoff). Instead, they are supposed to use a simplified writing system with fewer characters, known as *onna-de* ("women's hand"), and to use it only for letters and diaries.

But attempts to control what people read and write can produce unforeseen results. Several classics of Japanese literature have been written by women of the Heian times. Lady Murasaki's *The Tale of Genji* is one. So popular are her Genji stories – so real and psychologically complex does she make her vain, self-centered, but irresistible prince and his various lovers – that even men read *Genji*. One is the regent, Fujiwara no Michinaga, the father of the emperor's Number One Wife. Michinaga is probably the most powerful man in Japan.

In fact, it was Michinaga who hired Lady Murasaki to be a teacher and companion to his daughter, Empress Shoshi, and to give her private lessons in Chinese poetry. When Lady Murasaki arrived at court she began to keep a journal of court life. That is how we know that, one day, the normal order of court life has been disturbed: a stranger has gone through her things. This intruder has not taken anything of value. Her silk robes patterned with silver threads are still stored in their wooden boxes. Her fragrant aloe-wood combs; her special containers of cloves and musk and sandalwood, with which she blends her own incense; her brushes, inkstones, and supply of Chinese paper are all untouched. Only *Genji* is missing.

Lady Murasaki suspects Lord Michinaga himself. "While I was busy attending to Her Majesty, His Excellency came quietly into my room and found a copy of *The Tale* that I had brought home for safekeeping," she writes in her journal. "He may have given it all to his daughter. I no longer have the master copy, and I am afraid that the rough version she now has may hurt my reputation."

Lady Murasaki cannot challenge Michinaga openly; in this era, Japanese women have no power. If he asks what is troubling her, she will try to prompt him to confess.

Her opportunity comes on a soft morning as she sits with her screen shutters open, looking out at the mist hovering over the empress's formal gardens. She hears a footfall on the path. Suddenly she sees Lord Michinaga plucking some flowers, then heading in her direction. She retreats modestly behind the paper screen that forms a wall of her room. But there's no stopping him when he wants something. He tosses the flowers over the screen to provoke her into responding. "Give me a reply!" he commands.

Lady Murasaki is taken aback, but only for a moment. She pulls out her inkstone and brushes and writes something about the dew doing too much honor to the mere flower. She passes him the piece of paper. He studies it, reading her poem as a coded message: "Why are you, the dew, favoring me, of all people, with your attention?"

Lord Michinaga requests her brush and writes a response. The dew, he writes, cannot help where it falls. The flower, however, can accept the dew by showing whatever color it wishes. His poem means that she has more power than she admits.

Then he boldly looks behind the screen to study her reaction. She picks up her fan in self-defense. The women of Heian Japan understand that the rules of etiquette are a kind of protection. Like paper screens and paper fans, they may not be sturdy, but they do set limits.

Fujiwara no Michinaga, normally the most confident of men, wonders if this literary lady is angry at him. Does she know that he has ordered his servant to "borrow" her manuscript? Lady Murasaki's dark eyes glance knowingly at him from above the brim of her fan. He can read her *Tale of Genji*. But she will not let him read her face.

The Pillage of Baghdad

SOME OF THE world's greatest books can no longer be read. They have been destroyed by those who wanted to destroy a civilization's voices, its stories, its ideas, the very memory of its existence.

The extraordinary library at Alexandria, founded after the death of Alexander the Great, was ravaged many times. When Julius Caesar sailed into the harbor at Alexandria to help Queen Cleopatra, he torched the ships of her enemies and the flames leapt ashore, sending about forty thousand papyrus scrolls of the old library up in smoke. In the fourth century AD, a Christian mob tore apart the library – and several librarians who were trying to guard the books. In 641, when Caliph Omar – a leader of the new Muslim faith – arrived in Alexandria at the head of an army of converts, he is said to have stopped in front of the ancient library and told his warriors, "If what is in those books agrees with the Word of God, then the books are not required. If they disagree, they are not desired. Therefore, destroy them." The Chinese emperor Shi Huang-di was a great book-burner in the second century BC. In the 1500s, in Mexico, Bishop Landa burned hundreds of precious books of the local Maya people, saying they were filled with "superstition and the devil's falsehoods." Five hundred years later, as we shall see, Adolf Hitler took his turn at the bonfire.

But amid all this ruination of books, one atrocious act of vandalism stands out from the rest – the orgy of sheer destruction that wrecked one of the greatest centers of ancient, classical, and Muslim learning in the world. It happened in the spring of the year 1258. "Hardly ever has Islam survived a more disastrous and mournful event than the destruction of Baghdad," wrote a Muslim scholar of the time. "Never in history had a civilization suffered so suddenly so devastating a blow," the American historians Will and Ariel Durant wrote in 1950, seven centuries after the crime.

Medieval Baghdad was more than a city. It was a world cultural capital, like New York or Paris today. It was the city where storytellers compiled *The Thousand and One Arabian Nights*, where mathematicians developed algebra and the concept of zero. Its libraries contained collections of ancient Greek and Persian and Hindu manuscripts. It was the center of Islamic culture, and made Europe's cities at the time seem primitive and illiterate by contrast. "Blessed be Baghdad, seat of learning and art/ None can point in the world to a city her equal," the Persian poet Anwari wrote in the 1100s. "Her suburbs vie in beauty with the blue vault of the sky. . . . And thousands of gondolas on the water/ Dance and sparkle like sunbeams in the air."

In 1258, Sunni and Shia Muslims, Christians, Jews, Zoroastrians, and other sects from all over Asia – more than a million people – lived in Baghdad. It was home to poets, philosophers, librarians, scribes, scientists, doctors, mathematicians, translators, and students at the public university. Before its enemies struck, the city had around thirty-six public libraries, more than a hundred booksellers, and countless book collectors. One Baghdad doctor refused an invitation from the Sultan of Bokhara because, the doctor explained, it would take four hundred camels to move his book collection. If the doctor was still in Baghdad in 1258, he must have regretted that decision.

Because the Mongols were coming.

These alarming warriors lived in the grasslands of Central Asia, where since the dawn of time they had had nothing but their flocks of sheep and goats, their horses, their freedom, and their bravery. Around 1200, a single Mongol warrior, Genghis Khan, suddenly decided to conquer the world. The Khan's Mongol hordes were almost irresistible; they destroyed kingdoms from Poland to China. And they were contemptuous of the people they conquered – fools who had lost the taste for riding wildly across the plains, fools who preferred to live like fat sheep penned up in smelly cities. Once, someone asked Genghis Khan, "What is the greatest happiness in life?" He replied, "To crush your enemies, chase them before you, steal their riches, see their families weep, ride their horses, and carry off their wives and daughters."

Genghis Khan made sure that his sons and grandsons would carry on this happy work. On one occasion the old man took his grandsons – young Kublai, eleven, and his little brother Hulagu, nine – out hunting. Kublai, fast and alert, shot a darting rabbit. Little Hulagu brought down a slower but bigger target – a goat. Their conqueror grandfather called them over and smeared the blood from the boys' first kill on their faces.

The family believed it was destined to rule the world. To prepare the boys, their mother, a Christian named Sarkhaktani, arranged for Kublai to have a Chinese tutor. For young Hulagu she arranged Christian teachers from Persia. In 1252 the Mongol hordes gathered to decide the fate of Asia, and all agreed: Kublai would rule China, while Hulagu would subjugate the lands from Persia to Egypt. "Treat with kindness and good will any man who submits," Hulagu was told. "Whoever resists you, plunge him into humiliation."

Hulagu and his army rode south into Persia, accompanied by siege engineers (experts in besieging cities) sent from China by his brother Kublai, and reinforced with troops of Christians keen to strike a blow against Islam. He destroyed the castle fortress of Alamut, home of the fearsome Muslim sect known as the Assassins. Then, in 1257, he sent word that Baghdad should surrender.

This Persian miniature painting shows the Caliph of Baghdad, al-Mustasim, being brought before Hulagu. The Mongol invader killed most of the city's Muslims, but spared some Christians because his own mother was a Christian.

The city's ruler, Caliph al-Mustasim, and his advisers just laughed at Hulagu's threat. Surrender? Ridiculous. The Caliph of Baghdad was one of the most powerful men in the Muslim world. In theory, he could summon a million warriors from his Muslim allies to fight for him. As well, he had sixty thousand troops of his own. Alas, Caliph al-Mustasim was a fool who preferred to practice his beautiful calligraphy rather than drill the city's troops. The caliph had no idea that his own vizier was already in secret communication with Hulagu – or that some of Baghdad's Christians were discussing deals with the Mongols.

The caliph dismissed Hulagu's delegates with the message "By what counsel, what armies, and what lasso will you bring a star [me] into your bonds?" As the Mongol messengers walked out of Baghdad, ordinary people pummeled them and jeered at them. The messengers reported these insults to Hulagu. Enraged, the Mongol warrior sent a final warning. The caliph, who was starting to sense danger, replied that the city would surrender after all. But he refused to do so in person.

Have it your way, said Hulagu.

The Mongols arrived on the outskirts of Baghdad in January 1258. First, Hulagu lured the city's defenders into a marshy area, where his men opened a dike so that waters of the Tigris River trapped and drowned them. Next, his Chinese siege engineers began smashing Baghdad's walls with huge battering rams, and his catapults bombarded them with boulders. This went on for a month. The people of Baghdad cowered inside the shaking walls, but no one came to their rescue. By February 4, the walls had been breached.

The caliph surrendered three days later. Baghdad trembled for a week, while the Mongols waited like tigers on a leash. Then Hulagu gave the word. His warriors grabbed their curved bows, their axes and swords, and put on their helmets of leather hardened with lacquer. Below them lay the great city, its treasuries, palaces, parks, and pleasure gardens bordering the glinting river. The Mongols hoisted their small round shields. The hour had come.

Some say the sack of Baghdad went on for a week, some say it lasted forty days. Carpets and pillows were slashed; so were people. It is said that two hundred thousand people were murdered, and their heads piled in pyramids, but some reports say more than a million died. Scholars and poets were cut down in the streets. There were reports that so many scrolls were thrown into the Tigris River that the water ran black with ink. Other reports said so many libraries were dumped into the water that the Mongols could ride their horses across on the ruined books.

The Mongols left most of Baghdad in ashes and rubble. Fifty years later, travelers to the city found that the caliph's personal library, though empty, was still standing, in the midst of a ruined palace and a garden completely overrun with weeds.

Even other Mongols were shocked by what Hulagu had done to Baghdad. His own son Teguder converted to Islam, and changed his name to Ahmad. His cousin Berke Khan, a convert to Islam, became his mortal enemy.

As for the monster himself, after his job was done, he turned his horse back to Mongolia, which he preferred to the cities of the south. While his generals and army marched on to Damascus, Hulagu spent his later years studying astrology.

But Hulagu's attack had some curious results. Like many Mongols, he had a passion for almanacs, pamphlets of astrological forecasts. Mongols also loved gambling with playing cards. Both the cards and the almanacs were often printed with wood blocks, using technology imported from Kublai Khan's domains in China. As the Mongol conquests brought a kind of peace to Asia, trade routes opened up, and these printed objects were traded to the West. In 1265 two Italian travelers, Niccolò and Maffeo Polo, came through Mongol lands. They were given safe passage from Hulagu's realm to Kublai Khan's court in China. Kublai Khan, a more civilized man than his brother, told Niccolò and Maffeo that his mother had been Christian, and he asked the Polos to carry a message to the Pope in Rome.

Six years later the Polo brothers returned to the Mongol court in China, taking Niccolò's young son Marco with them. Marco noted how the Mongols used block printing to make things like cards and paper money. He also observed that they were always checking their astrology texts "to see in books how the sky stands now."

Marco Polo wrote an account of his adventures, *The Travels of Marco Polo*. Although it's not clear how much of it is true, his reports of the treasures of the East inspired European explorers to look for easier trade routes to Asia. When Christopher Columbus sailed to America in 1492, hoping to reach the Indies, he carried a copy of Marco Polo's *Travels* with him.

So while the Mongols wreaked destruction, they also helped open up the world to trade and travel between East and West. Perhaps their printed almanacs and paper money found their way to Europe – because the idea of printing certainly did.

Still, when you attack writers and poets, chances are good they will attack you back. They will turn your name to mud in the history books. And Hulagu, when he is remembered at all, is mostly remembered as the monster who turned a city of wonders into a wasteland.

8

Giving Books to the People

FOR THOUSANDS OF years, ordinary people couldn't read books because they were rare and expensive. Suddenly a new invention made it possible to mass-produce books cheaply. Then the problem wasn't finding books; it was controlling them.

This is the story of two men who both had a brilliant idea, an idea that would revolutionize the world and the way we think and learn.

Both men were born around 1400, on opposite sides of the world. One was the King of Korea, popular, powerful, respected, rich, and able to command the resources of his country to carry out his idea. Yet his name, Sejong, is unknown to most of the world. The other was a commoner who spent much of his life in debt, working in secret. He often got tangled up in lawsuits, so he seems to have been a prickly character. Yet it was this man, Johannes Gutenberg, whose name became synonymous with the idea they both had: printing with movable type.

The process of printing by carving a whole page of text into a wooden block and then inking the block and stamping it on paper had been around for a long time, but it was time-consuming and inconvenient. Both

The earliest known portrait of Johannes Gutenberg may not look like him: the artist, André Thevet of Paris, did it more than a hundred years after Gutenberg's death.

Sejong and Gutenberg, independently, came up with a better idea. What if you didn't have to create a separate block for each page? What if you could just go to a box and choose individual metal letters to build a sentence, then another, until you had a whole page, and then use those letters again to build the next page? That way, you could print many more books than had ever been printed before.

The idea was first tried in Korea. This mountainous land of cool pine forests where ginseng grows lies between China and Japan, and has always had to struggle for its independence from both its neighbors. Back in the 1400s, Korea's royal family was also at war with itself. Sejong's grandfather, King Taejo, had had two wives, and the sons of the first hated the sons of the second. Sejong's father, Taejong, had come to the throne after the murders of at least two of Sejong's uncles.

Korea had adopted the ideas of the Chinese moral philosopher Confucius, who had lived almost two thousand years earlier. The Confucian tradition took reading and learning seriously, and all royals were supposed to attend lectures, write poems, and respect scholars. But young Sejong, perhaps retreating from his family's troubles, read all the time. Once, his father the king ordered a servant to remove all reading material from the prince's quarters. One book fell between the screens and wasn't noticed. Prince Sejong found that one book and, according to legend, read it a hundred times.

In 1418 King Taejong was worried about Japanese pirate attacks on his southern coasts. He decided to step down from ruling his country and concentrate on defending it. But who would become king in his place? His eldest son, Crown Prince Yangnyong, was notorious for drinking too much and chasing other men's wives, and had been sent into exile. The middle son had become a priest.

So Taejong, splendid in his dragon robes and seated under his red parasol of kingship, summoned his youngest son into the throne room. The bookworm Sejong arrived, walking under the blue parasol of a prince. His father told him it was time for him to accept the king's red parasol.

"Your Majesty, I am unworthy to receive this," Prince Sejong begged. "Please take it back."

The king refused. Mounting his sedan chair, he ordered his men to carry him out of the palace. For days Sejong sent letters begging his father to return. Taejong was adamant. The reluctant Sejong became king.

From the beginning, King Sejong showered favors on a group of people who would ultimately betray his dreams: the intellectuals, who were mostly followers of Confucius. To please them, Sejong banned their rivals, Buddhist monks, from Korea's capital city, Seoul. To further please the Confucians, he also established a center of learning, called the Jade Hall of Scholars, where twenty of the country's most respected men were brought to study undisturbed. It is said that, when it got very cold, the king ordered that they be draped with his own fur-lined robes.

Though the king honored and protected his scholars, he knew that Korea must grow stronger to be able to stand up to its powerful neighbors.

He dreamed that his people, from doctors to farmers, might be taught to read, so they could learn how to be wiser and more skilled. In 1403 his father had established a foundry to make bronze characters in order to print books – an idea that had been around for a while in China, Japan, and Korea – but the results were sloppy. To secure the letters in their proper order the printers used beeswax, which kept melting. The lines of type slid sideways, and the print was blurry.

And there was a bigger problem. Korean writers were using Chinese characters, which are whole words or parts of words, rather than letters of an alphabet. Any serious printing operation would need thousands of characters. Not only did this make printing complicated; King Sejong suspected that few of his subjects would have the time to learn all those Chinese characters.

He commanded his old tutor and two young scholars to consult writers of other languages and develop a new, simple system. In the twenty-fifth year of Sejong's reign, the king proclaimed that Korea had a new alphabet. As well, he wrote a book, *The Correct Sounds for the Instruction of the People*, in which he explained that those who cannot put things into words cannot express their feelings. "I have been distressed by this and have newly designed a script . . . which I wish everyone to practice. . . . A wise man can learn it in a morning."

King Sejong called this alphabet Hangul. Its twenty-eight letters (later simplified to twenty-four) were designed to show the position of the tongue when producing the sounds. The alphabet was easy to learn and easily cast in individual bronze letters. But how could the bronze letters be lined up and fixed in place to produce neat pages? According to legend, the king himself solved the problem; in a dream he saw that the edges of the metal letters could simply be fitted into one another. No more sloppy beeswax. On waking, he explained his vision to his printers.

Among the first books to be printed in Hangul and in movable type were *The Ode to the Flying Dragon in Heaven* (a royal family history) and

Moon Shines on a Thousand Rivers – a poem King Sejong wrote in honor of his wife Sohun, who had just died.

The scholars in the Jade Hall did not like what the king was choosing to print. Sejong's poem was also a Buddhist prayer – this from a king who had earlier taken their advice and banned Buddhists. Nor did the scholars like the idea of printing books in the Hangul alphabet. Led by the respected, stubborn senior scholar Choe Mal-li, they presented their objections to the king. They said: Abandoning Chinese characters is a political error because it will offend our huge and powerful neighbor China. They said: Abandoning Chinese letters is in bad taste because it means we are behaving like Manchurians, Mongolians, and Japanese, who are barbarians. Besides, they said, if everyone studies this new alphabet, within a generation there will be no more scholars who can read the old Chinese classics.

What all these objections added up to was: If you bring in this simple new system that anyone can learn, then we, with all our years of study, may be out of a job.

Over the years, Sejong had grown old and half-blind from a life of reading. Since his beloved wife had died, he had found more comfort among Zen Buddhist monks than among his quarreling Confucian scholars. When he built himself a small Buddhist chapel, the scholars staged a strike and walked out of the Jade Hall.

King Sejong died in 1450. After his death, little by little, the pro-Chinese Confucian traditionalists forced Korea back to the old ways. As the court slipped once more into intrigues and civil wars, Sejong's descendants were driven into exile. Within a hundred years, Hangul had been downgraded to an alphabet used mainly by women for household lists. For the next four hundred years, Korea's printers used only Chinese characters. Until the 1800s, when Hangul was readopted for official use by Korean nationalists, Sejong's idea of mass copies of easy-to-print, easy-to-read books in the Korean language was a lost dream.

But on the other side of the world, in Germany, it was a different story.

In 1418 – the year Prince Sejong became king of Korea – Johannes Gensfleisch Gutenberg was still studying at university. He was from a family connected with the mint (coin-making operation) in the German city of Mainz. It was probably hard for scholars to concentrate on Latin and religious training at that time, for the Christian Church was in chaos. There were three "popes" claiming to be the true Pope, and everyone was quarreling. If only there was a way to unify all Christians, and bring people back to the Word of God!

In the 1430s – as King Sejong was sending his team out to investigate alphabets – Gutenberg was still trying to figure out what to do for a living. Because Mainz was on a route through which pilgrims passed on their way to Rome and the Holy Land, and because his family worked at casting metal coins, he came up with the idea of manufacturing pilgrimage badges of stamped metal, with mirrors encased in them. Legal papers from 1438 show that Gutenberg went into business with two partners to corner the pilgrim souvenir-mirror market.

Bad luck; that year there was an outbreak of the plague, and the 1439 pilgrimage was called off. The partners took him to court, according to Mainz city documents. However, Gutenberg convinced his investors to stay with him for something really big, a mysterious project he was working on at a foundry (metal-molding factory) just outside of town. He not only got these partners to agree to lend him more money; they also promised in writing to keep this unknown project a secret.

When one of the partners died, his heirs said Gutenberg had to take them on as new partners. Gutenberg refused, so they all went to court once more. The heirs claimed that Gutenberg was so afraid the court would force him to reveal his secret project that he had ordered the destruction of equipment at his foundry "so that none shall see it."

What was going on at the foundry? What was the "it" he wanted no one to see? We can guess. Late into the night, sweating in the glow of his metal furnaces, Gutenberg was trying to use his skill in casting metal to cast letters of the alphabet.

First, he figured out how to make multiple copies of the most frequently used letters. That way the printer would always have enough Es and Os. Next, he designed several versions of these letters, so that when fat letters like W and E occurred next to thin letters like I, the spacing would not be we i rd. Once the letters were lined up into a block of text, he figured out what kind of ink should be applied so that when the letters were pressed against paper, the ink neither spread out nor smeared but stuck to the paper evenly.

By 1448 – well after King Sejong started to publish Hangul books – Gutenberg was still experimenting. Records in Mainz show that he was borrowing money from more people just to keep going. In 1449, he borrowed 800 guilders at 6 percent interest from a businessman named Johannes Fust.

As partners go, Herr Fust was pretty patient. Gutenberg's project made no money in 1449, or the next year or the next. Impressed by Gutenberg's work, Fust kept investing more money. By 1455, though, he decided that matters weren't moving ahead fast enough. He convinced Gutenberg to take his son-in-law, Peter Schoeffer, into the business as an apprentice. Once Schoeffer knew how the invention worked, Fust was ready.

With Schoeffer as his witness, Fust took Gutenberg to court and sued for the total he had invested, about 2,000 guilders (more than $250,000 in today's money). In court, Gutenberg finally revealed what he was up to. He explained to the judge that he had not been stealing his investors' money; he had simply been plowing it back into *das Wercke der Bücher* (the work of the book).

In Europe, mass-producing books was an idea whose time had come. In 1453 the Muslim Turks had taken over Constantinople, the stronghold of Eastern Christendom. In fear, Constantinople's Christian scholars had grabbed their books – from Greek classics to Armenian Bibles – and had fled to the West. Suddenly, all over Europe, people wanted to read about ideas that would save Christianity and Western civilization.

But although there was a growing market for books, there was no way to produce them quickly. It took two scribes five years to do one edition of

This 1676 engraving by Abraham von Werdt (you can see his initials at the center top and bottom left) shows how large and complex early printing-publishing operations were, and how much space was devoted to storing pieces of type.

a 1,200-page book. Fust and Schoeffer correctly judged that mass-producing books was a good way of getting rich. When Fust won the court case against Gutenberg, he must have thought his fortune was made. He was named sole owner of the print shop and what Gutenberg was manufacturing there: the world's first printed Bible, manufactured by means of movable type.

The Gutenberg Bible finally appeared in 1456. Johannes Gutenberg's name is not on it, because of the court case, but it was created by his process and to his design – and what a thing of beauty it was. There were 35 copies printed on vellum (white calfskin), and 150 on imported

YOU CAN'T READ THIS

Italian paper. Each page displayed two rectangles in Gothic typeface. The letters of the Latin text were crisp, and so carefully spaced that whether there were as few as twelve words in a line or as many as fifteen, the lines always ended as evenly on the right margin as on the left. Gutenberg Bibles, now valued at tens of millions of dollars, are collected by the world's greatest museums.

By the 1460s, the problems between Gutenberg and Fust were dwarfed by a bigger concern: war. The Church wanted to recapture Constantinople from the Turks, and the Pope demanded a huge tax to pay for this adventure. Then he doubled the tax. The Archbishop of Mainz refused to pay, and issued a printed pamphlet – possibly produced by Gutenberg – explaining why. The archbishop's act of rebellion enraged local nobles who were loyal to the Pope. By 1462 Mainz was encircled by soldiers calling out for the blood of heretics – that is, anyone who didn't support the Pope and the Catholic Church.

The leader of the siege, a nobleman named Count Adolf, sacked the city, seizing the property of those who had resisted. Gutenberg escaped to nearby Eltville and started a new printing operation. Three years later, Count Adolf decided that he needed Gutenberg's skills, and tried to make peace. The count offered "our dear, faithful Johannes Gutenberg" a pension, an annual allowance of two thousand liters of wine, and the promise to "clothe him . . . like one of our noblemen." So Gutenberg was able to work in comfort for the last three years of his life. When the master printer died in 1468, his body was taken back to Mainz and buried with honor.

For the next generation or two, some Europeans still resisted Gutenberg's invention. Realizing that printing presses would put them out of business, a group of scribes convinced the King of France to ban printing presses from Paris. But the ban was never enforced. The European publishing industry had taken off too fast.

Why did the idea of printing stall in Sejong's world and move ahead in Gutenberg's?

Because in Korea the invention had come from the top down. When later kings came to power in Seoul, they suppressed Sejong's idea of teaching ordinary people to read. Instead, they went back to tradition: elite scholars, ignorant peasants.

In Europe, though, the dream grew from the bottom up, starting with entrepreneurs and businessmen. If one business disappeared, there were more to take its place. In Korea, the people who most loved books wanted their ranks to stay small and special. By contrast, the learned men and leaders of Europe were horrified by the loss of Christian lands to the Muslims. They thought it was a good idea to have multiple copies of the Bible, in Latin, in everyone's hands, so everyone could cherish and protect the Word of God.

By the time church and political leaders realized how dangerous mass-produced books could be, it was too late – much too late – to put a stop to them.

Darkness upon the Deep

READING HELPS PEOPLE think for themselves. After printers started producing copies of the Bible, people started thinking more about religion. But some of their ideas were different from what the Church expected.

Peter Schoeffer Jr. looked carefully at the man who had just entered his shop, in the German town of Worms. It was 1525, and anyone who worked in the politically charged business of printing could not be too careful. People were always trying to control what was being printed, and printers were being thrown in jail, or executed.

The man at the door was short, slight, English, with a worn but intelligent face. He looked like a priest, which in fact he was. But he was also a fugitive, on the run from the agents of Henry VIII, King of England. Although Schoeffer realized that letting this small man into his shop would put himself in danger, he let him in.

In 1525 the printing business was still young. Schoeffer's father, Peter Schoeffer the elder, had been Gutenberg's apprentice, and his grandfather had been Gutenberg's partner, Johannes Fust. Yet the industry those men had started was already tangled up in Europe's angriest religious and political battles. A German priest named Martin Luther was writing books challenging the corruption of the Catholic Church, and the authority of the Pope in Rome. Luther's books were banned and burned across Europe and England. But they were also being read. Some estimates are that, by 1521, as many as 300,000 copies of Luther's work had been sold across Europe.

The little English priest told Schoeffer that his name was William Tyndale. He spoke German well – he'd studied at the university in Hamburg, and heard Martin Luther there. Was he a follower of Luther? Tyndale denied it. But he had the same basic mission: to open religion up to ordinary people; to let them read the Bible in their own language and think for themselves about its message.

Of course, there had been Bibles in languages other than Latin for centuries – the Armenians had produced a Bible over a thousand years earlier. But in Europe, popes and kings rightly suspected that if you put easy-to-read Bibles in the hands of ordinary people – including women and peasants – they might notice that the Good Book never said that popes and cardinals and kings should be able to tax the peasants in order to live in palaces. Reading and thinking about the Bible might cause people to challenge authority – to go the way of Martin Luther, and break with Rome. And now this Tyndale was saying that he had translated the Bible into English. No wonder powerful people wanted him dead!

Tyndale told Schoeffer that his translation was already half printed. The job was being done by a printer named Peter Quentel in the city of Cologne. Unfortunately, Quentel was also printing church propaganda (the word "propaganda" comes from the Latin phrase *propaganda fide*, "promoting the faith") for a man called Cochlaeus, who'd turned up in Quentel's printing shop to supervise the work. There, Cochlaeus overheard two drunken printers boasting that England – Catholic for so many centuries – would soon be Protestant.

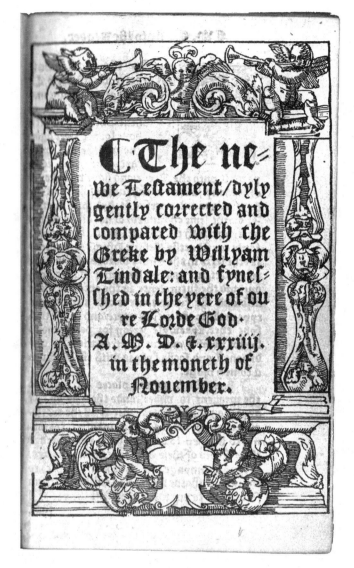

Just four editions of William Tyndale's New Testament survived the bonfires of English censors and the ravages of time. This title page of one edition shows how spelling used to be more variable (note the name Willyam Tindale).

What's this? thought Cochlaeus.

Pouring the printers more wine, he asked them what they were talking about. The printers blabbered that they were preparing three thousand copies of the New Testament in English. They said the money for the job was coming from English merchants, who would be smuggling the finished Bibles back into England. Cochlaeus took this alarming news and went straight to Cologne city hall. In short order, armed guards raided the print shop – but someone must have warned Tyndale, for he had already slipped away with his half-printed book.

And here he was at Schoeffer's door in Worms. Would Schoeffer complete the job? Schoeffer said yes. The money was good. So was the quality of the work; Tyndale, who'd studied Greek and Latin and theology (religion) at Oxford and Cambridge, had translated the New Testament into graceful, simple English. And he wasn't finished; he told Schoeffer that his next project was to learn Hebrew so he could translate the Old Testament as well.

You've come to the right town, said Schoeffer. There was a lively Jewish community in Worms, where Tyndale could probably find a Hebrew tutor.

Thanks to movable-type technology, the job went quickly. Some of Tyndale's New Testaments reached England by the spring of 1525. By Christmas of that year, English people were being thrown in jail for owning them.

Among all those in England's church and political leadership who wanted to crush Tyndale's translation, the most ferocious was Sir Thomas More, a devout Catholic and one of the country's most learned men. Like Tyndale, More was a writer. His novel, *Utopia*, is about a traveler who stumbles into a wonderful society of tolerance and co-operation. But More also wrote church propaganda and, like many writers, he believed that he should stand by what he wrote – not, alas, *Utopia*, but these stern religious tracts. Normally a sane and humane man, More wrote that Tyndale was "a hellhound in the kennel of the Devil." By 1529, More was Lord Chancellor of England – the highest-ranking official in the country.

Henry VIII found it useful to let Sir Thomas More attack heretics. The king needed to please the church authorities, because he was in the process of asking them for a major favor – a divorce from Queen Catherine of Aragon, who had failed to give him a son, and permission to marry Lady Anne Boleyn. The Church did not recognize divorce – but surely, for a king, a way could be found?

Lady Anne, the king's new favorite, read what she liked. She liked Tyndale's book *The Obedience of a Christian Man* and recommended it to King Henry, who announced, "Why, this is a book for me and all kings to read." In 1531 the king sent a secret agent, Stephen Vaughan, to Germany to find Tyndale and beg the fugitive priest to return to England.

Hunting down Tyndale took some doing; he'd been living in hiding, dodging the agents of the Church since 1525. But finally Vaughan was able to convince Tyndale to meet with him to hear the king's offer of safe passage back to England. Tyndale's response was skeptical. He understood that Henry VIII might like his books, but the king might like even more the idea of using Tyndale as a pawn in his game with the Church over questions of divorce and remarriage. Tyndale also knew that men like Sir Thomas More hated him. He told Vaughan that he appreciated Henry's promise but feared that his enemies would advise the king, "Promises made to heretics need not be kept."

Annoyed by Tyndale's refusal to return, Henry hardened his heart against him. He was used to getting his own way. In 1533 – the year he married Anne Boleyn – he sent out secret agents to kidnap Tyndale and bring him back to London. The next year, Henry VIII declared the Act of Supremacy, rejecting the Pope and making himself head of the Church of England.

Tyndale kept slipping away from the king's agents' nets. Hunted across Northern Europe, he was shielded by people willing to risk their lives so he could write his books. Some merchants gave him a safe, warm place to study and work; others kept an eye out for church agents; still others smuggled his books back to England, hidden amid heaps of skins, or tucked away in false bottoms of crates. In England, Sir Thomas More kept building bonfires of these Bibles, and publishing whole books attacking Tyndale, comparing his writings to the plague. Yet despite More's best efforts – or maybe because of the attention – more English people read Tyndale's works, and more sent money.

And all the time Tyndale was in hiding, he kept up his work of translating, writing, and being published. He even published his translation, from the Hebrew, of the Pentateuch, the five books of Moses in the Old Testament. This was a job he loved; "The properties of the Hebrew tongue agreeth a thousand times more with the English than with the Latin," he wrote.

Finally, in 1536, in Belgium, the hunt ended. Ignoring warnings, Tyndale went one night to meet an Englishman named Phillips who had pretended to be his friend. It was a trap. The fugitive priest walked straight into the arms of soldiers waiting to arrest him. He was taken to Vilvoorde Castle, near Brussels. Despite the appeals of his many admirers in England and Northern Europe, Tyndale was executed.

Back in England, that same year, Queen Anne Boleyn was beheaded on orders of King Henry, who'd decided he wanted to marry Wife Number Three (he would have six wives in all). As for Tyndale's old enemy Sir Thomas More, he had publicly contradicted the king when Henry claimed to be the final authority on royal marriage. More's head had been chopped off too.

When printing first came to Europe, church leaders had hoped that mass-produced Bibles and other religious texts would bring people together. And they did – but not by ensuring that all readers believed the same thing. Rather, printed books led to standard rules of grammar, spelling, and vocabulary, so people could better express all the ways they disagreed with one another.

The great English books printed in the 1500s and early 1600s, including *Utopia* and William Shakespeare's plays, helped shape the English language.

Tyndale's death as depicted in Foxe's Book of Martyrs. *John Foxe, a Protestant, fled to Switzerland to escape a similar fate at the hands of English Catholic authorities. He didn't return until the Protestant Queen Elizabeth I took the throne in 1558.*

Tyndale's Bible was one of those language-shaping books. It introduced to the English language words that we now all know, such as "Passover" and "peacemaker," "scapegoat" and "long-suffering." Here's another word the long-suffering priest seems to have invented for his English Bible, for it occurs in no book published before Tyndale: "beautiful."

Seven decades after Tyndale's death, another English monarch, King James I, authorized a new translation of the Bible. The men who produced the King James Version turned to the translations of William Tyndale. It is estimated that as much as 80 percent of the King James Bible – the Bible most English-speaking Christians would rely on for the next four hundred years – is based on the words of William Tyndale, whose Book of Genesis – in its original odd-seeming spelling – begins: "In the beginnyng, God created heauen and erth. The erth was voyde and empty, and darckness was vpon the depe, and the spirit of God moued vpon the water."

10

The Cousins and the Code

WHEN TEXTS ARE written in code, they can only be read by someone with the key. With enough time and ingenuity, though, a good code-breaker can usually discover that key.

It was June 1586, and for the first time in many years the pale face of Mary, Queen of Scots, looked happy and hopeful. Although the Catholic queen was being held prisoner at Chartley Hall, a stately home deep in the English countryside, her friends had smuggled her a letter in code from people in London and France who supported her cause. After her private secretary, Claude Nau, decoded the letter, which was in English, he read it to her in French – Mary always felt far more at home in French than in English or Scots English. On hearing the message, for a brief spring afternoon the prisoner queen allowed herself to dream.

Mary dreamed she would be able to escape the house arrest imposed by her cousin, Queen Elizabeth I of England – daughter of Henry VIII and Anne Boleyn, and now head of the Church of England. Mary dreamed of a mighty army coming from a Catholic nation to rescue her

P.Pailleu pinx. E.Scriven sculp.

MARY QUEEN OF SCOTS.

Mary had become Queen of Scotland upon her father's death, when she was just six days old. She was the granddaughter of Henry VIII's sister, and her cousin Elizabeth was Henry's last surviving child. If something happened to Elizabeth, Mary had the best claim to the throne. As it turned out, Elizabeth did die childless, and Mary's son became King James I of England.

and place her on the throne of England, so she could make the country Catholic once again.

The letter that arrived that June day was from a handsome, rich, daring young London merchant named Anthony Babington. Like Mary, Queen of Scots, Babington was a committed Catholic, and like Mary, he wanted to restore England to the Catholic Church. His letter reported that Spain would support Mary's claim to the throne. It spoke of plans to assassinate Queen Elizabeth.

Babington's recklessness, Mary knew, could get all the plotters into deadly trouble. But she felt confident that her cipher (code) could not be broken. Carefully she dictated her reply, in French, indicating that she was ready to go ahead. Her secretary translated the letter into English and then into the queen's special cipher.

This code looked like no known language. For the letter A there was a circle; B was a sideways H, C was a wedge, D looked like a picket fence. There were twenty-three letter symbols, plus thirty-six symbols representing frequently used words such as "send" and "with." Just to be sure the coded letter did not fall into the wrong hands, Nau sealed it in a watertight packet and hid it in a cask of beer. The barrel was shipped to London.

Mary wrote her letter on June 25. Babington did not receive it until July 6. In between, the unthinkable happened. Sir Francis Walsingham, Queen Elizabeth I's Principal Secretary – and spymaster – had been waiting to pounce on the Queen of Scots. His agents found the beer cask and intercepted the letter. Then Walsingham passed it to Thomas Phelippes, a genius at cryptanalysis (code-breaking).

Phelippes didn't look very impressive – he was of "low stature . . . eaten in the face with smallpox." But he was patient and clever.

To break the code, he used "frequency analysis." After determining which letters occurred most frequently in typical sentences, he checked which symbols were used most frequently in the code. For example, in English the letter E occurs more than twelve times for every hundred letters. T is likely to turn up at least nine times for every hundred letters, A eight times, and so on. Late into the night Phelippes kept at it, doggedly, patiently substituting the most frequent letters for the most frequent code signs – until at last words started to make sense.

It was only a matter of days. As soon as Phelippes could read Mary's letter, and understood that the prisoner queen had approved an assassination plot against Elizabeth, he went to Sir Francis Walsingham.

Walsingham could have arrested Mary on the spot. Instead, he decided to trap as many of the conspirators as possible. He let the letter go through to Babington, who wrote Mary back.

Mary's next letter to be sent by beer-cask delivery was also intercepted. This time, Mary asked the plotters not to murder Elizabeth until Mary

Sir Francis Walsingham's spies not only helped trap Mary, Queen of Scots; they also reported that Spain was planning to launch its Armada (a fleet of ships) to invade England in 1587. England was therefore prepared for the attack, and sent out small, fast fighting ships to set fire to the large, cumbersome Spanish vessels.

herself had safely escaped, so no one would take revenge on her. When Phelippes read this letter, he drew a little gallows as a sign to his master.

Yet Walsingham was still not ready to act. He knew that Phelippes, a man of many strange and unsavory talents, was also a master forger, so he told him to add a fake postscript to the letter – in Mary's secret code, of course – asking Babington for more details. It read, "I would be glad to know the names and qualities of the six gentlemen which are to accomplish this designment . . . for it may be that I shall be able, upon knowledge of the parties, to give you some further advice. . . ." Then this letter too was resealed, put back in the beer cask, and sent on its way.

Babington replied to the doctored letter, never suspecting a thing. Following what he believed were Mary's orders, he sent her, in code, all the names he thought she had asked for. Now Walsingham was satisfied.

Queen Elizabeth had no choice when faced with all the evidence Walsingham presented to her. Mary was found guilty of treason. The English queen postponed her execution several times – Elizabeth had a horror of beheadings, since her own mother had lost her head to the axeman – but eventually she ordered her cousin's death.

Mary, Queen of Scots, was very dignified as she walked to her beheading. Her ladies-in-waiting walked beside her, and her dog, too. After the beheading, the little dog refused to leave Mary's body. Elizabeth is said to have cried when she heard the news of Mary's execution. But after all, Mary had been plotting to do the same thing to her. Besides, Elizabeth had promised to protect her country against foreign powers. And – who knows? – the plot might have succeeded, but for the work of Tom Phelippes, a man who refused to accept that there was any code that could not be broken – or anything that could not be read.

Books Not to be Read

SOONER OR LATER, we come across a book that we decide we should not read because we think it is false or dangerous. But do we have the right to make that decision for other people?

On a long summer day around the year 1620, three boys – Big Magnus, Little Bogi, and their friend Eirikur, the cleverest, bravest boy in all Iceland – went searching for a book of magic. In those days, most boys their age in mainland Europe could not even read, but in Iceland, isolated in the midst of the North Atlantic, learning and writing were prized. On long winter nights, when the darkness closed in and the sheep huddled in the barns and the fishing boats stayed in port, there wasn't much to do but sit with a book by the fire.

Iceland became Christian in the year 1030, but for years it had a kind of Christianity that would have shocked people in mainland Europe. Icelanders tolerated people who kept alive the old pagan ways, who made herbal potions or chanted spells calling on the power of the Norse gods. By 1600 the Church got more strict about these pagan remnants, and possessing a book of sorcery was punishable by death. Yet even church leaders themselves were curious about those old ways.

In Iceland, summer night skies stay light, so Bogi, Magnus, and Eirikur weren't worried about darkness overtaking them as they set off across the hilly meadows. They were determined to find the magic book *Raudskinna – Redskin* – said to have been buried along with its owner, a strange old man who had lived alone with his cow, and who might have practiced the ancient ways.

"I've heard this book *Raudskinna* was written at the Black School," Eirikur told his friends.

"What was the Black School?"

"A place where wizards studied long ago," Eirikur replied over his shoulder. "There were no teachers . . . the students just said what they wanted to learn, and then they would enter a dark room, or maybe a cave. It was so dark they couldn't see anything – until books appeared, written in fiery red letters. The students had no other light, just letters lit from within."

Bogi the curious asked, "Reading in the darkness?"

Big Magnus pushed him violently. "You fool! They were magicians!"

But Eirikur had another explanation. "Everyone who is ignorant reads in darkness. Then they become . . . enlightened."

At last Eirikur stopped by the entrance to an old churchyard. The tombstones cast long shadows in the mauve evening light. Bogi shuddered, and Magnus said softly, "Maybe we should not be looking for this book."

But Eirikur was full of daring. "What if the book is real?" he said. "What if it has power, knowledge that we can use to do good – find lost sheep, foretell storms, stop fishermen from getting drowned at sea . . . ?" Pushing on into the churchyard, he scanned the tombstones, looking for the hermit's grave.

Suddenly Magnus cried out. Someone was approaching: a stranger with hollow eyes, leading a cow on a rope. Under his arm was a huge book bound in red leather.

"!" breathed Eirikur.

"Here," said the old man, with a strange smile. Giving Eirikur the book, he melted away into the deepening shadows.

The Enchanter Merlin (imagined here by the American artist Howard Pyle) was the powerful adviser to the legendary King Arthur. Merlin's personal book of magic was said to have been passed on to other wizards, and is itself the subject of poems and stories.

The boys wrapped themselves in cloaks of animal skins and tried to keep warm as Eirikur read in the twilit northern night, page by page.

Finally the sky began to brighten again. "Morning?" asked Bogi, shivering.

Eirikur looked up. He was just coming to the last pages. He slammed the book shut and looked around.

The old man had come back. He was smiling.

Eirikur thrust the red-covered book at him. "Take it!" he cried.

The old man's smile dropped away. He looked shocked, as if Eirikur had denied him some prize. Furiously he tucked away the old book. Then he seemed to vanish.

Eirikur was very quiet, and he let Big Magnus lead the way home. The three boys walked in silence. Finally Bogi could no longer help himself. "What did you read?" he blurted.

"Just enough," Eirikur told him. "Enough to know that if I had read any further, I would have lost my soul to the Devil."

There are many versions of the story of the magic book *Raudskinna* and Eirikur, a real person who lived in the 1600s and later became a famous Christian bishop. What really happened in Eirikur's search for knowledge, we have no way of knowing. But the legend of *Raudskinna* is not only a version of the struggle between Iceland's old religion and the new; it is also a way of telling of each reader's struggle to judge whether the contents of a book are evil or useful.

This struggle has gone on since the dawn of the written word. In 1559, just before the time of Eirikur, the Vatican issued its *Index Librorum Prohibitorum*, the Catholic Church's official list of forbidden books. On the list were Martin Luther and William Tyndale, and books thought to contain magic. One, *The Book of Secrets of Albertus Magnus*, was actually just a collection of herbal remedies compiled by a helpful monk around 1250. But by 1605 those herbal remedies looked like satanic potions, and *The Book of Secrets* went on the index.

The Index Librorum Prohibitorum *listed books that Catholics were not supposed to read. Of course, for some people this only made those books more tempting. There was also an* Index Expurgatorius, *which listed books that Catholics could only read if certain passages were changed or deleted.*

Even in our own time, some people fear that books about magic really have some unhealthy power. J.K. Rowling's story of a student wizard, *Harry Potter and the Philosopher's Stone*, has had the weird distinction of being the most challenged book in library and public school collections in the United States. In Canada, after an uproar at the Durham Region School Board near Toronto, school officials sent home consent forms for parents to sign before their children could open a copy of *Harry Potter*.

We should take the censors seriously. Of course, they are wrong to fear Harry Potter, who, after all, is a good person who stands by his friends and tries to defeat evil. But the censors are right to respect the power of books, and to remind us all that books contain forces we may not fully appreciate. Ultimately, though, each reader – like young Eirikur – has a responsibility to know when to shut the covers.

That Dreadful Mr. Shakespeare

THE JOKES PEOPLE laughed at two hundred years ago would shock us now. But we find it funny to look at what they found shocking – and what they tried to prevent other people from reading.

By 1790, the majority of the people in England could read and write. This meant that strange and upsetting ideas were within their grasp. Farmers and tradespeople were reading newspapers and books about revolutions in the United States and France, and about how the French had chopped off the head of their king. Women were opening romantic novels and discovering new ideas about love and marriage. A few were even reading feminist books like Mary Wollstonecraft's *A Vindication of the Rights of Women*.

As for children, who knew what mischievous ideas they were picking up from books?

One of the world's first stores to sell children's and family books had opened in London in 1744, at the east end of St. Paul's Churchyard. The man who owned this store was also a publisher, John Newbery (an American children's book prize, the Newbery Medal, is named after him). Newbery designed books especially for children, on sturdy paper with

Mary Lamb, the writer who fatally stabbed her mother in a fit of insanity. She and her brother worked together to write Mrs. Leicester's School, *and collections of stories for children, as well as* Tales *from* Shakespear.

pleasing illustrations, books that he sold with the promise that they would "make Thomas a good boy and Polly a good girl."

One of Newbery's most popular books was Anna Laetitia Barbauld's *Lessons for Children*, which told young readers: "Do you know why you are better than Puss? Puss can play as well as you . . . she can run as fast as you, and faster, too, a great deal. . . . But can Puss talk? No. Can Puss read? No. Then that is the reason why you are better than Puss – because you can talk and read. . . . If you do not learn, you are not good for half as much as Puss. You had better be drowned." Nowadays, no children's publisher would dare to suggest that either a child or a cat should be drowned – which just goes to show that what people consider shocking changes over time.

In 1807, two new books appeared in print; perhaps they even turned up on the shelves at Newbery's shop. The books were *Tales from Shakespear* and *The Family Shakspeare* (people then spelled the playwright's name many different ways). Both these books rewrote William Shakespeare's plays to make them more "suitable" for impressionable readers. Yet both these books had dark secrets of their own.

In the first case, it's easy to see why there was secrecy. The title page of the first edition of *Tales from Shakespear: Designed for the Use of Young Persons* falsely declares the author to be the well-known poet and essayist Charles Lamb, and the publisher to be one Thomas Hodgkins. In fact, the publisher was really William Godwin – and his name cast fear in the hearts of English citizens everywhere. Old, bearded Mr. Godwin was a famous political radical, a socialist. His late wife had been none other than the feminist writer Mary Wollstonecraft, and their daughter, Mary, would grow up to write the novel *Frankenstein*.

As for the author of this book – it was true that Charles Lamb had written six of the chapters, but most of the stories, fourteen to be precise, had been written by Charles's sister, Mary Lamb. Her name could not be mentioned because, in a fit of insanity, she had committed murder.

Some of England's best poets and writers, including Samuel Taylor Coleridge and William Wordsworth, knew Mary Lamb as a dear friend.

However, they also knew that she was subject to fits. One afternoon in September 1796, she had picked up a carving knife that was about to be used on the family's roast mutton dinner, and plunged it into her mother. Charles had grabbed his sister from behind, forcing her to drop the knife. Then she had been taken away.

At that time the King of England, George III, was subject to spells of insanity. Because the English people were learning to tolerate this in their king, they were becoming more understanding of mental illness generally. So Mary Lamb was not executed for her crime, but merely sent to a madhouse. After a year she seemed sane again and moved back home with her brother, who promised to take care of her. Her fits came back every other year or so. Whenever Mary felt another spell of madness coming on, she and Charles could be seen walking across London, back to the madhouse, crying as they carried Mary's straitjacket between them. Whenever Mary got better, she came home and started back to work, writing with Charles.

With a murderess author and a publisher who was a notorious radical with feminist connections, it's easy to see why *Tales from Shakespear* was presented with less than the whole truth. But what about the other book? What dark mystery kept the real author of *The Family Shakspeare* a secret? What could possibly be as bad as revolutionary politics, feminism, or murder?

At the front of *The Family Shakspeare*'s first edition, an anonymous preface explained that the author was trying to serve "those who value every literary production in proportion to the effect it may produce in a religious or moral point of view. . . ." The author had "omitted many speeches in which SHAKSPEARE has been tempted to purchase laughter at the price of decency." With all the cheap laughs censored, said the writer, the plays could safely be read by "young persons of both sexes."

Over the next few years, it leaked out that the book was the work of Thomas Bowdler, a retired doctor of strong religious beliefs. After *The Family Shakspeare* appeared, Dr. Bowdler's name eventually became so well

YOU CAN'T READ THIS

THE

FAMILY SHAKSPEARE,

IN ONE VOLUME.

IN WHICH
NOTHING IS ADDED TO THE ORIGINAL TEXT,
BUT THOSE WORDS AND EXPRESSIONS ARE OMITTED WHICH CANNOT
WITH PROPRIETY BE READ ALOUD IN A FAMILY.

BY THOMAS BOWDLER, ESQ., F.R.S. & S.A.

—— EXEMIT LABEM, PURUMQUE RELIQUIT
ÆTHEREUM SENSUM, ATQUE AURAI SIMPLICIS IGNEM.
VIRGIL.

THE ELEVENTH EDITION.

LONDON:
LONGMAN, BROWN, GREEN, AND LONGMANS.
1855.

Despite all the effort he spent chopping up Shakespeare's work, Thomas Bowdler admired the playwright. Bowdler declared that, thanks to his "improvements," Shakespeare's genius "would undoubtedly shine with more unclouded lustre."

known that it turned into a verb. "To bowdlerize" means to prudishly muti-late a text, to delete all the bits you disapprove of.

But maybe Thomas Bowdler shouldn't get all the credit. We now think there was another bowdlerizer behind the scenes.

Thomas, his brother John, and two sisters, Jane and Harriet, were the children of a truly talented prude, Squire Bowdler, who liked to read aloud to his family, making up corrections to Shakespeare and other great English authors as he went along. Thomas recalled those evenings with great fond-ness, and said his father did such a flawless patch-job that no one suspected a thing. Coming from such an ultra-respectable household, the Bowdler children were very sensitive to anything that offended modesty. When John grew up, he used to advise women to watch what they said about babies and bodies. "Few women have any idea how much men are disgusted by the slightest approach to these [topics] in any female," he warned.

Then there was Thomas, who hung around literary London and boasted in his letters that, as a young man attending a public reading, he had once sat near Samuel Johnson, the author of the great dictionary. Thomas trained to be a doctor but, as with all the Bowdlers, anything to do with bodies – sick people, for example – made him squeamish, and he quit medicine. At age fifty-two, he got married. Maybe his wife's body repelled him too, for the couple soon separated.

The younger Bowdler sister, Harriet, was so proper that when she went to the opera (according to a letter written by an acquaintance) "she kept her eyes shut the whole time, and when I asked her why, she said it [the dancing on stage] was so indelicate, she could not bear to look."

Whoever had written it, *The Family Shakspeare* of 1807 had gotten rid of the entire tragedy of *Romeo and Juliet*; no more wickedness about teenagers who fall in love and marry against their parents' wishes. You could not read *Othello*, the great tragedy about a black military hero who murders his white wife after he is falsely convinced that she has been unfaithful – how disgraceful! In *Hamlet*, the hero's sexy flirtation with Ophelia was trimmed. *Macbeth* lost the scene in which a drunken porter imagines being a porter in hell. And "damned Glendower" in the play *Henry IV* became "vile Glendower."

A second edition of the bowdlerized Shakespeare was published in 1818. This time Thomas Bowdler's name was on the title page. This time the cleanup job was more thorough. *Othello* was allowed back, but only with strong misgivings; as Dr. Bowdler warned in a letter to *The British Critic* magazine, "The subject is unfortunately little suited to family reading." Shakespearean characters of loose morals, like Doll Tearsheet, had disappeared (her way of speaking, Dr. B. explained to *The British Critic*, "is in the highest degree disgusting"). In the original version of *Henry IV*, Prince Hal laughs at his drunken friend Falstaff: "Thou art so fat witted, what with drinking of sack, and unbuttoning thee after supper." That's cut down in the Bowdler version; it was thought indecent for poor old Falstaff to loosen his tight clothes after a big meal.

The 1818 edition of *The Family Shakespeare* (with a modern spelling for Shakespeare's name this time) was noted by two influential magazines, which started a public battle over whether its censorship was a good thing or not. *Blackwood's Magazine* called the Bowdler book "prudery in pasteboard," and fought publicly with the *Edinburgh Review* (which described the book as "this very meritorious publication"). All the publicity convinced ordinary book-buyers to check out the new Shakespeare for themselves.

And so the next edition, printed in extra-large type so families could read it easily by candlelight, became a bestseller. For the next century and more, *The Family Shakespeare* sold steadily and inspired many imitators. By 1900 there were almost fifty different versions of sanitized Shakespeare on sale, but the Bowdler version remained at the head of the pack, and stayed in print until the middle of the 1900s. Generations went through school not realizing that they were reading the classics filtered through 1820s notions of respectability.

Or that those notions were, at least at first, the notions of Harriet Bowdler. We now suspect strongly that it was Harriet – she who could not look at dancing – who first cleaned up the Shakespearean sewer. A letter written in 1811 by a friend of the family, the Reverend Robert Mayow, refers to "Mrs. Bowdler's Shakespeare." There is also an 1821 letter from a bishop who seems to have been in on the secret. He notes that "Mrs. Bowdler and her Brother have done a great deal towards moralizing Shakespeare." And after Harriet died in 1830, her nephew Thomas wrote a letter revealing that "The Shakespeare is my aunt's edition. . . ."

But the lady herself never admitted to anything. She wrote another anonymous book, *Sermons on the Doctrines and Duties of Christianity*, which was also a bestseller (it went through fifty-two printings over fifty years). In it she insisted, "I do not write for fame but in the humble hope of being useful to a very respectable class of my fellow Christians." But that was not the real reason she would not put her name on *The Family Shakspeare*. The truth was simple: Harriet did not want it known that a woman of her refined sensitivity had actually read Shakespeare's original words. And she certainly didn't want people to realize that she *understood* what she read – lewd puns, dirty jokes, and all.

13

A Book at His Fingertips

READING IS A complicated process of seeing and recognizing symbols, and translating them into sounds and words. Problems with the eyes or the brain can make that process seem impossible. But it's amazing how some people refuse to allow anything, even blindness, to stop them from reading.

Louis Braille, born in 1809 in the village of Coupvray, France, was just three years old that day when he toddled into the workshop of his father, a saddle-maker. No one was there. He saw his father's tools – the knives and awls kept razor-edged to cut the saddle leather – gleaming by the big wooden workbench. The little boy decided to use these wonderful instruments the way his father did, slashing and slicing to make grown-up things. He reached for the shiniest, sharpest tool, grabbed a piece of leather, and poked it. He wasn't sure if the tool had pierced the leather, so he held the leather up to look, and poked again.

His mother heard terrible screaming. Running to the workshop, she found that her child had stabbed himself in the eye. Frantically she bandaged him and applied herbal remedies, but Louis's eye grew infected. He probably rubbed it, because the infection spread to his other eye. The little boy went blind.

This bust of Louis Braille stands in the Bibliothèque Nationale (National Library) in Paris. Although his reading and writing system is almost two hundred years old, and simple enough for children to start learning by the age of five, the world still does not have enough Braille teachers and materials.

Many blind people lived terrible lives in those days, begging on street corners for a few coins. People made fun of the blind as they turned round and round, unable to see who was tormenting them. Louis's parents were determined to spare their bright little boy such a lonely, empty life. They convinced a teacher to let Louis attend the local school, and the boy memorized his lessons so well that he often stood at the head of the class. His father cut letter shapes out of leather for him, and his older sister Catherine fashioned letters from pieces of straw. But since Louis could not read, it was clear that, as the lessons became more complicated, sooner or later he would have to drop out of school.

The teacher suggested that the family take the boy to a special school for the blind in Paris. A local nobleman, the Marquis d'Orvilliers, offered to pay the costs. And so Louis, not yet eleven, boarded a stagecoach with his father in February 1819, for Paris. Their journey ended at the front doors of the Royal Institution for Blind Children, on Rue St. Victor.

It was a legendary building, the former home of Saint Vincent de Paul, the great French religious figure who helped the poor and the sick, and most of the building was at least two hundred years old. During the French Revolution it had served as a prison for priests, and some priests had been put to death in the courtyard. To a sensitive child, the building probably felt haunted. Louis could hear the school's halls echo with the distant sound of coughing. But it was one of the world's most advanced schools for the blind, and while he was there Louis would change the world.

After the pleasant, grassy smells of the French countryside, the school must have appalled Louis with its stench. Its walls were frigid and damp to the touch. The fifteen stoves that burned through the winters could not keep the students from catching colds and worse. An 1821 government report on the place admitted, "The house is situated in a low-lying district which is airless, evil-smelling and conducive to the spread of disease." At that time no one knew about germs, and how they made people sick.

But the good part was this: There were almost sixty other blind children to talk with, and specially trained teachers to help them memorize lessons in arithmetic, geography, history, and literature. Best of all, there were books – huge books with the print pressed into thick paper so that the letters stood out on the other side, and blind students could pass their hands over the raised surfaces and read the letters by feeling them.

Louis soon realized that these books weren't very good. Of the fourteen books printed with these raised letters, most were grammars; not one was a storybook. Students had to feel each letter and remember it, and go on to the next and remember it, until they had the whole word – and do that for each word in the sentence. Also, the letters had to be so big that the books were very awkward to handle. Like his fellow students, Louis found reading difficult and slow. Music lessons were much easier. His fingers learned to fly across the keys of the organ and piano, and up and down the neck of the cello.

One day when Louis was in his early teens, the whole school was summoned for a special assembly. The children heard the director announce a special visitor: Captain Nicholas-Marie-Charles Barbier de la Serre, a French army artillery captain from an aristocratic family. The captain had just returned from America with an idea that might help the children.

While on the battlefield, the captain told them, he had developed a unique system of writing so that soldiers could send messages at night, when it was too dark to read. Captain Barbier's system let the soldiers feel paper coded in combinations of raised dots and dashes that represented syllables or chunks of sound.

As the students murmured with interest, the director explained that the school would be trying out Captain Barbier's system, both for reading and – using a little machine that pressed dots into paper – for writing as well.

Louis was one of the first to learn the system. It worked far better than those heavy books with the pressed-in letters. But it wasn't perfect, not for the needs of blind students. Some syllables were coded in as many as twelve dots – a lot for a reader to feel. Because the captain's dots and dashes only represented syllables, they didn't show spelling, accents (which are crucial in French), or punctuation. This was hardly surprising, since the system had been designed for battlefield dispatches.

Louis asked to meet with the captain, and suggested improvements. With his aristocratic background, Captain Barbier may have thought the saddler's boy was being uppity, daring to correct him. In any case, the soldier couldn't see why blind people would want to read anything more complicated than a battlefront bulletin. He refused to even think about making further refinements.

So Louis went off to design his own system. After class, working late into the night – he didn't need light anyway – he experimented with a pointed stylus, poking dots into paper. He decided the dots should represent letters instead of syllables. And instead of Captain Barbier's complicated system of twelve dots, he shrank his clusters to blocks of six dots or fewer. This meant that each letter could be felt all at once, with one touch of the fingertip, just as sighted people see a whole letter at a glance.

Louis Braille worked for three years on his invention. Finally, he presented the school director with the system he had invented. For blind people all over the world, yearning to read books for information, for education, and for sheer pleasure, Louis's system would open the doors to a vast and wonderful library.

Within another three years, Louis Braille had published a Braille grammar book. Then came a book titled *Method of Publishing Words, Music and Plain Songs by Means of Dots, for Use by the Blind and Arranged for Them.* Pretty good for a youth not yet twenty.

However, the cold, old, smelly school where Louis was by now working as a teacher was starting to kill him. The foul air infected his lungs. Before he was thirty years old he was coughing up blood, a sign of the deadly disease tuberculosis.

Louis Braille died on January 6, 1852, just after his forty-third birthday, and was buried in Coupvray. A hundred years later, his body was moved to the Pantheon, a huge, temple-like building on the Left Bank in Paris, where he lies with other heroes of France. A bronze bust of him, commissioned by the villagers of Coupvray, stands in the village where he was born. It shows a gentle, handsome man with his head tilted slightly downwards, as if he is concentrating on hearing some quiet message. His hands, which he turned into tools of reading, remain to this day in a small urn in the town cemetery.

The rest of the world didn't adopt Louis Braille's system right away. For years, many schools refused to ask blind people what system they preferred. Educators refused to accept the idea that reading with your fingertips might (as we now know) involve a slightly different part of the brain than reading by sight.

Braille was only accepted in England after authorities let blind students vote on which system to use. It wasn't until 1878, at an international congress to adopt a printing method for sight-impaired people, that Austria, Belgium, Britain, Canada, Denmark, France, Germany, Italy, the Netherlands, Sweden, and Switzerland agreed that Braille would be their standard. The United States took another forty years to sign on.

Even now, people are still fighting over different forms of Braille. Symbols for dollar signs and e-mail addresses vary from country to country. At the beginning of the twenty-first century, a blind scientist who learned Braille math in Canada or the United States could not read a British math text, and a blind British mathematician could not read math texts in Braille from Germany. "It's still a real Tower of Babel," says Darleen Bogart, a past president of the International Council of English Braille.

Despite these blind spots, Louis Braille's system has opened up millions of books – novels, school texts, histories, mysteries, even nursery rhymes, in more than fifty languages – to people who can't see. The boy from Coupvray, whose life seemed blighted by that one childhood accident, succeeded in putting the world of reading at their fingertips.

14

Freddy the Slave Boy

IN THE DAYS before the Internet, radio, and TV, reading gave people access to the larger world. So the best way to keep them ignorant was to forbid them to read. But that was easier said than done.

Freddy was eight years old when he was introduced to Tommy. Tommy was then aged two. Both boys lived in the American state of Maryland, in 1826. But Tommy was white and Frederick Augustus Washington Bailey was brown. Freddy was a slave, and little Tommy was his new master.

Freddy had come from the plantation of a white man named Captain Aaron Anthony (some people whispered that the captain was Fred's real father). The slave boy hardly knew his mother, Harriet. When he was tiny she had been sent to work in the fields. Freddy had been brought up by his granny.

A slave's life was brutal. Before he was eight, Freddy had seen the captain whipping people, including the boy's own cousin Hester. All the slaves feared the master's anger, but not as much as they feared being sold, which meant being taken away, probably forever, from all their family and friends. Being sold was what had happened to Freddy's sister, his aunts, and seven cousins.

Now some relatives of Captain Anthony, Hugh Auld and his wife, Sophia, had asked if they could use Freddy to look after their little boy, Tommy. Frederick, just a piece of property, had arrived at the Aulds' home in the city of Baltimore, frightened and alone.

At first the Aulds were good to the eight-year-old. Instead of an old corn bag, which was what slaves used for blankets out on the plantation, they gave Freddy a straw bed and a blanket; instead of ash cakes (rough cornmush baked in the embers of the fire) he had bread and porridge. His new masters even gave him shoes and trousers, so he could go out in public and run errands across town.

His new mistress seemed kind. She read aloud to Freddy and Tommy from the Bible. Her voice, Frederick later remembered, was "mellow, loud and sweet." He was entranced. He asked his mistress to teach him to read. Of course, she said.

They began with the alphabet. He absorbed that quickly, so they went on to simple words of three and four letters. Soon the slave boy could pick these words out of the Bible. Wonderful! said the mistress. Then she made a big mistake. She boasted to her husband that young Freddy could almost read.

Hugh Auld's rage was terrible. Behind it there was fear – fear that the whole rotten system of slavery could come tumbling down if the dark-skinned workers ever got hold of the power that goes with reading. Years later, Frederick wrote that the white man had screamed at his wife, "Learning will spoil the best nigger in the world!" and added, "He should know nothing but the will of his master and learn to obey it!" Frederick also wrote that his master's ranting "stirred up not only my feelings into a sort of rebellion, but awakened within me a slumbering train of vital thought." Hugh Auld's determination to keep his slave ignorant gave Frederick the determination to educate himself.

The Aulds weren't the only obstacle in Freddy's way. Some states had laws forbidding slaves to learn to read. Owners knew that if slaves read all those posters advertising for the return of runaways, they'd realize that escape was possible. Worse, they might read about human rights, or about the abolitionist movement, which aimed to end slavery altogether. Or they might learn that in 1803–1804 the slaves of Haiti had risen up, driven out their masters, and established a free *black* republic.

Virginia, Georgia, and North and South Carolina passed laws in 1829 and 1831, threatening fines, whipping, and imprisonment for anyone teaching slaves to read. Any black people who were found to be able to read would have a finger cut off, so they wouldn't be able to write. In 1831, a Virginia slave named Nat Turner led a rebellion that left more than sixty white people dead. Nat Turner could read. For some frightened slave-owners, that confirmed it: They would have to crush any signs of reading.

Scalded by her husband's fear and anger, Mrs. Auld tried to harden her heart against Freddy and his dreams. "Nothing appeared to make my poor mistress more angry than seeing me, seated in some nook or corner, quietly reading a book or newspaper," Frederick recalled years later. "I have had her rush at me with the utmost fury, and snatch from my hand such newspaper or book, with something of the wrath or consternation, which a traitor might be supposed to feel on being discovered in a plot by some dangerous spy." The Aulds would send little Tommy hunting for Freddy, to make sure he wasn't sneaking in time with a book.

So Frederick had to find other ways of learning. There were white boys on the streets of Baltimore who would give him a short lesson if he brought them a biscuit from the Aulds' house. There was an old black man in the neighborhood, a Christian named Charles Lawson, who liked to read the Bible with Frederick and let the boy try to read it to him. And there were tough kids down by the shipyards who were unwitting accomplices. With a piece of chalk, Freddy would scrawl the letters he already knew on the pavement and then dare the white kids to "beat that if they could." They'd write more letters, Frederick would copy the new letters, and the game would go on.

When Master Tommy was old enough to go to a real school – for white children only, of course – he brought home his copybooks and left them lying around. Frederick quietly stole them away to a hiding place in the attic. If anyone found him, he knew, he would be whipped. But the risk was worth it. Crouched in the attic late at night, he rewrote the lines Tommy had written in school, making his letters look as much like Tommy's as possible.

Because Frederick was good-looking and bright, people in the Aulds' neighborhood would get him to run small errands. Sometimes they'd pay him with a shiny coin. By age thirteen, the slave had earned enough money to go out and buy a book. For fifty cents he bought himself a copy of *The Columbian Orator*.

Sometimes a lucky reader finds a book that reassures him that he is not alone, and not crazy. This was one of those books.

Inside were speeches by famous men such as the Roman orator Cicero, and Daniel O'Connell arguing for Catholic Ireland's freedom from England. If these essays excited Frederick, he was even more startled to find that his book contained a dialogue between a master and his slave; the slave convinces the master that it is wrong to "own" another human being.

The Columbian Orator was like a match; it lit a fire in Frederick's mind. The boy took to reading newspapers he found blowing in the gutters of Baltimore. He learned about the abolitionists. He learned that there were states to the north, and the British colony of Canada, where slaves could be free.

When Frederick was fifteen, his owners suddenly informed him that he would be leaving Baltimore to work on a farm owned by Hugh's brother Thomas. The country Aulds were even meaner than the city Aulds. There was less food, more beatings. Frederick hated this new life. He refused to call Thomas Auld "master." His owner sent him to a "slave-breaker" to be beaten into submission. This man, a Mr. Covey, whipped Frederick so often that the slave's shoulders were scarred for life.

One day, Frederick hit Covey back.

Covey stopped cold. He realized that if he killed the young man, he would have to pay Thomas Auld for lost property. If he went to the police, and people heard that a slave had hit the slave-breaker, he would lose his slave-breaking business. So Covey backed off. He said nothing. He quietly delivered Frederick back to his owner.

In 1836, the eighteen-year-old Frederick and some friends tried to run away, but they were captured. Two years later, Frederick tried again. Borrowing some official documents from a free man, a black sailor he'd met in Baltimore Harbor, he boarded a train for the north. Whenever a white person questioned him on that long train ride, he showed the sailor's papers. When he got off the train he was in the free city of Philadelphia, in the free state of Pennsylvania. Before the year was out, he had married a free black woman named Anna and had changed his identity. Gone was Bailey, a name that was probably on runaway-slave posters all over Baltimore. He chose a new name, that of a hero in Sir Walter Scott's *The Lady of the Lake*: Douglass.

This new free man, Frederick Douglass, found a job as a manual laborer and started teaching other ex-slaves to read. Because he used language so beautifully, people asked him to make public speeches against slavery. In the 1830s, 1840s, and 1850s, those sorts of speeches could get you heckled and beaten. Frederick Douglass ignored the insults and even the occasional beatings. He became a public-speaking star.

Over six feet tall, he cut a memorable figure, reported a Swedish writer. He had "an unusually handsome exterior . . . those beautiful eyes were full of dark fire." He was "forcible, keen and very sarcastic," said a Massachusetts newspaper. "He talks as well, for all we could see, as men who have spent all their lives over books."

Before long, he tried writing books himself. His first, *My Bondage and My Freedom*, was published in 1855. It told of his early life, of the beatings

As well as being a writer, a news-paper publisher, and a brilliant public speaker, Frederick Douglass was part of the Underground Railroad, the secret network that helped slaves escape to freedom. He did all he could to end slavery.

on the plantation, the Aulds, the slave-breaker Covey. My *Bondage* became a bestseller in America and Europe, and went through nine editions in England alone. Frederick Douglass toured Scotland, Ireland, and England, speaking to halls packed with thousands of people. (By this time, slavery had been illegal throughout the British Empire – including Canada – for over twenty years.)

In 1847 the Douglass family had moved to Rochester, New York, another free state. Here, with financial backing from white abolitionists, Frederick launched a newspaper, *The North Star*. This newspaper carried essays, columns, and editorials by Douglass, excerpts from novels by Charles Dickens, and in 1848 an announcement of a meeting at Seneca Falls, New York, to discuss voting rights for women. Douglass went to Seneca Falls, one of a handful of men in a sea of women's faces. He stood and made a speech in favor of giving women the right to vote. Of all his causes, he later wrote, the fight for women's rights gave him the most pride: "When I ran away from slavery it was for myself; when I advocated emancipation, it was for my people; but when I stood up for the rights of woman, self was out of the question." He added proudly, "I found a little nobility in the act."

Slavery did not end easily in the United States. Although the Emancipation Proclamation of 1863 declared slavery illegal, many people remained enslaved until the end of a bloody civil war, in 1865. Even after that, most black people remained trapped in poverty. Many were still abused, and almost all were shut out of the best jobs and opportunities.

In the last years of his life Frederick Douglass was often disillusioned and angry. But he was also often triumphant. The former slave who had struggled so long and so ingeniously to "learn his letters" became the American ambassador to the black republic of Haiti, and a faithful champion of black and women's rights. If you ever visit the city of Rochester, New York, you can see an image of this man who taught himself to read by daring other boys to write letters on the sidewalk, and by chasing scraps of newspaper down the streets. There's a bronze statue of Frederick Douglass taking tea with the feminist Susan B. Anthony. The two appear to be deep in discussion about how to make this a better world.

The Two-Faced Treaty

TRANSLATION LETS US read what was written in another language. But it leaves us at the mercy of the translator. As the Armenians discovered long ago, an alphabet that spells the sounds of one language may not work for another. In the same way, a language that expresses the thoughts of one culture may lack words that are vital to another. In that case, how can the translation ever be accurate?

The tall brown man, his face marked with blue tattoos, strode purposefully up the grassy slopes of Flagstaff Hill. That was the name New Zealand's *pakeha* (white British settlers) had given it. The Maori warrior knew the place by other names. Looking down, he could see Kororareka, a little port town on the North Island of New Zealand. Its streets were famous for rum shops, taverns, gun-toting adventurers, brawls, and women of bad reputation. Missionaries called Kororareka the hellhole of the Pacific. New Zealand's first surveyor-general had reported that it was "a vile hole, full of impudent, half-drunken people."

The view of the town no doubt disgusted the tall warrior, whose name was Hone Heke. His people, who had lived in New Zealand according to their code of honor for centuries, had a purer and more beautiful image of their country, Aotearoa, the Land of the Long White Cloud.

Hone Heke, flanked by his wife, Harriet, and the warrior Kawiti, portrayed by Joseph Jenner Merrett. As an artist, Merrett helped document Maori culture; in his other job, as a land surveyor, he helped undermine it.

Hone Heke turned his eyes away from the town, fixed his gaze for a moment on the flagpole on the hill's summit, and then swung his axe. His first blow caused the flagpole, and the Union Jack that flapped atop it, to shudder. The man reared back and swung his blade again and again. Down crashed the flagpole and the flag of Her Majesty Queen Victoria, ruler of the British Empire.

This was not the first time that Hone Heke had chopped down the Union Jack at Kororareka. As far as the British settlers were concerned, if Hone Heke provoked them again, there would be war. As far as Hone Heke was concerned, it was time for payback – payback for the land grabs by *pakeha* settlers, payback for the imprisonment of Maori warriors, for the loss of local trade because the white government had raised taxes – and most of all, payback for the broken promises of the Treaty of Waitangi, which had promised one thing in its Maori text, and something different in the English version.

All over the world, as European settlers and traders moved in on other cultures, they brought pieces of paper that they urged local people to sign. These papers – treaties, proclamations, contracts of purchase – gave the newcomers land. Often, the local people couldn't read the papers. Too late, they learned that what was written there supposedly allowed the Europeans to fence off farms, build towns, cut down trees, hunt and fish and generally take over. As for the promises the Europeans signed to repay the local people, they didn't seem to be worth the paper they were printed on.

This was the experience of aboriginal people in Canada, the United States, Africa, South America, and all around the Pacific. It's a story that is still unfolding in many places in our own time. It is still unfolding in New Zealand, the island nation founded by the Treaty of Waitangi, one of the world's best-documented examples of a treaty that changed in translation.

Hone Heke had been at the original signing of the treaty on February 6, 1840, at Waitangi, near Kororareka. The signing had been celebrated by 1,500 Maori men performing the *haka* – the traditional war dance, like a series of karate moves, which ends with the warriors making ferocious faces, bulging their eyes and sticking out their tongues fearsomely. He knew that the Treaty of Waitangi had been signed in two languages, English and Maori, by chiefs and by British officials resplendent in their plumed hats.

Only 39 chiefs knew enough English to read and sign the English version. Most signed the Maori version. (The translation had been done

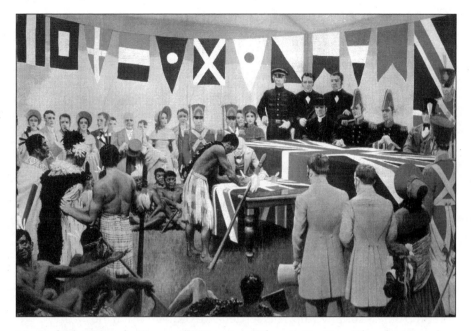

Maori chiefs signing the Treaty of Waitangi on February 6, 1840. Though many others signed the document at later dates, the anniversary of this first signing is celebrated as Waitangi Day, New Zealand's national birthday.

by English missionaries.) At Waitangi and eventually across New Zealand, about 450 Maori chiefs had signed or put their marks on the agreement. Whenever Maori expressed doubt about the wisdom of signing, the missionaries reassured them that the treaty would protect them from greedy settlers and drunken whalers coming ashore and stealing their fish and their women. Reassured by his missionary friends, one Maori leader, Nopera, explained to his people, "*Ko te atakau o te whenua . . .*" – "The shadow of the land goes to the Queen [of England], but the substance remains with us."

But this was not what the treaty said in English. The missionaries had overlooked the fact that some ideas simply couldn't be translated. While the English treaty gave Queen Victoria all "rights and powers of sovereignty" over New Zealand, the Maori treaty gave her "*te kawanatanga katoa*," the right to govern their lands. The difference? When you vote a government into office, you're telling them to do a good job – not to take over the ownership of your house.

Hone Heke, who had been taught to read and write by missionaries, actually supported the treaty that day in 1840. No wonder he (and many others) felt betrayed by what happened next. The treaty said Maori could only sell their lands to the government, usually at a low price. Yet the settlers could sell land to one another – so Maori had to sell their land cheaply and then watch as the value kept going up and up. Sometimes settlers started surveying Maori land even before the government was finished playing middleman. At the South Island community of Wairau, in 1843, an armed clash left four Maori and twenty-two settlers dead.

As the violence rose, emotions got uglier. Some of the settlers were rude and contemptuous toward New Zealand's original people. One, Joseph Somes, summed up the settlers' arrogance when he wrote, "We have always had very serious doubts about whether the Treaty of Waitangi, made with naked savages . . . could be treated by lawyers as anything but a praiseworthy device for amusing and pacifying savages for the moment."

In July 1844, Hone Heke staged his first public attack on the symbol of British rule; he chopped down the flag on the hill overlooking Kororareka. The British put it back up and, by the way, informed everyone that Kororareka was now to be called Russell. Hone Heke attacked the flagpole again. Back up it went. After the embittered chief axed it a third time, the British tried to sheath the pole in metal to protect it.

Hone Heke's rage was unabated. He'd been talking to Americans in town about their revolution, and had taken to flying the American flag on his war canoe – a reminder that British colonies that were mistreated could always rebel. On March 11, 1845, he and an ally, a respected old warrior named Kawiti, took action again. While Kawiti and his men went to the town and created a diversion, Hone Heke went back up Flagstaff Hill. Perhaps he stripped off the metal sheath. In any case, when the townspeople looked up, they saw their flag and flagpole crashing down a fourth time.

The white people knew that this defiance meant war. Most of them panicked and fled. British ships offshore fired on Kororareka. Dodging cannonfire, the warriors raced through the streets and looted some of the stores and homes. In the evening the sky was reddened by flames as the "hellhole of the Pacific" was set on fire.

The Northern War was now underway, and Hone Heke was a marked man. Yet he, Kawiti, and other rebel chiefs outsmarted the mighty troops of the British Empire time and time again. Armed with guns, many Maori turned out to be brilliant guerrilla warriors. They lured the British troops into ambushes and fired on them from the undergrowth. Good at mimicry, they would yell phony commands in perfect English accents to confuse enemy soldiers. Pretending to be drunk, they lured the *pakeha* into more ambushes. Knowing how appalled the Europeans were by the old Maori tradition of eating the flesh of their enemies, they taunted the British with calls of "Put the fat boys in front!"

The British were dismayed. Their losses were higher than they had expected, and the Maori were proving to be very good at engineering trenches and fortifications that could withstand British guns. How could mere natives beat British troops? For twenty years the skirmishes raged on. Hone Heke died in 1850 of tuberculosis, a disease brought to the islands by the settlers. Only after his death was a flagpole again raised on the hill overlooking Kororareka. In the end, Maori warriors weren't defeated so much as overwhelmed by the sheer numbers of *pakeha* settlers who kept arriving on their shores.

For more than a century, Maori kept up their fight by other means – demonstrations, court challenges, protests, occupations, and political activism. Finally, in 1975, the New Zealand government established the Waitangi Tribunal. Its job was – and still is – to study both versions of the treaty, and to decide on problems resulting from the differences. For example, if a Maori family own a parcel of land, does that mean they own what is under the land – mining rights? Do they own all the fish in the rivers that flow through their land?

Hone Heke, by John Alexander Gilfillan, a Scottish art professor who emigrated to New Zealand in 1841. He drew this in 1846. The next year, his wife and three of his children were killed by Maori, and Gilfillan left for Australia.

The tribunal hasn't ended the problems, but it has pushed things further toward a resolution than ever before. In 1995 Queen Elizabeth II, Queen Victoria's great-great-granddaughter, formally apologized to certain Maori tribes for breaches of the Treaty of Waitangi. If Hone Heke were still alive, would he be ready to let the flagpole stand? Would he be satisfied that all New Zealanders were trying to read and interpret the treaty in a fair way?

The Evil World of – Comic Books?

IT ISN'T ONLY words and ideas in print that can alarm the authorities. A new form of publishing may seem vulgar or revolutionary, or disrespectful, or attractive to the "wrong" kinds of people. If you think parents are worried about the Internet now, look at how worried some of them got about comic books in the mid-twentieth century.

Only a remarkable publication could be hated by two groups of mortal enemies, the Nazis and the anti-Nazis. Only something outrageous could provoke demands for censorship from Adolf Hitler, Benito Mussolini – and United States senators, and writers such as George Orwell (author of *Animal Farm* and *Nineteen Eighty-four*). Well, the politics of censorship makes for strange banfellows; all these people disliked comic books – and one in particular, *Superman*.

Adolf Hitler, the supreme ruler of Nazi Germany, came to power by beating up his enemies, killing them, crushing free speech, and burning books. Into the Nazi bonfires went the writings of the blind and deaf Helen Keller (because the Nazis thought disabled people dragged down the master race). Reduced to ashes were books by the science-fiction writer H.G. Wells, by Albert Einstein, by novelists such as Marcel Proust

Help! Danger!! Thousands in peril!!! The once-feared power of comics to depict violence and menace is now being harnessed to retell events from history. This page from the comic Explosion re-creates a tragedy that happened back in 1917. It shows a man trying to warn trains to stay away from Halifax Harbour, where a French arms ship loaded with TNT was about to collide with another ship. The two did collide, causing the largest man-made explosion until the atomic bomb.

YOU CAN'T READ THIS

and Emile Zola, and by the father of psychoanalysis, Sigmund Freud.

But Superman? Why hate the Man of Steel? Wasn't Hitler's whole crazy philosophy about Germans being a race of supermen with beautiful bodies? About the worship of strength and power? Superman barged through doors, grabbed guns from his enemies' hands, and ordered politicians to do whatever he wanted. Surely he was just the sort of person every young Nazi wanted to be?

For the Nazis, what mattered was not what Superman did, but what he was: a wise-cracking hero dreamed up by two Jewish American kids from Cleveland, Ohio. The man from the planet Krypton was a Jew! said Hitler's propaganda minister, Joseph Goebbels, waving a copy of the comic book in the German government headquarters, the Reichstag, in 1940. The Nazis wanted the Jews to disappear from Earth (and presumably from outer space as well).

But why did some Americans hate comics too? Why did they try to convince the United States Senate that comic books were ruining children's minds and morals?

Every time a new way of communicating opens up, it makes some people nervous. They sense that it will shake up the social order. The new Korean alphabet alarmed King Sejong's scholars in the 1400s; translations of the Bible frightened church officials in the 1500s; and in the 1800s, slave-owners tried frantically to stop their slaves from reading. In the 1900s, some people sensed bad influences rising from the pages of comic books.

The censors aren't being irrational. Ideas are powerful. And there are ideas, sometimes nasty ones, in comic books. Besides, some of the folks who published comic books back in the 1930s and 1940s really weren't the sort of friends you'd want your children to have. They were sleazy, cigar-smoking fellows with gangster pals. Superman's creators, Jerry Siegel and Joe Shuster, learned this the hard way.

Jerry Siegel was in his mid-teens when he met Joe Shuster at Glenville High, in Cleveland, around 1930. Both boys were what the school's most popular kids would have labeled losers. Jerry had no friends. His father, a tailor, had been murdered in a robbery at his shop, and ever since, his mother had sat at home in a black depression, while Jerry retreated into a geeky, nerdy world of science fiction and horror comics. When he wasn't reading trash, he was writing it. As for Joe, his family had moved to Cleveland from Toronto, Canada. Short, nearsighted, scrawny, he was into bodybuilding and drawing the kind of muscles he wished he had. Jerry and Joe met at the high-school newspaper and discovered that they both read pulp novels – Buck Rogers, Tarzan – and comics.

Comic strips had first appeared around 1894, when newspaper publishers realized they could sell thousands of extra copies by running drawings with stories and jokes. Right from the beginning, many parents didn't really approve of comics. Of course, this only made kids love them more. Those early comics were usually about kids with funny accents or slangy talk, who sassed the grown-ups and got into scrapes.

Then came the 1930s and the Great Depression. Around the world, businesses were shutting down; millions of people lost their jobs. Many felt angry and hopeless. Some turned to political protest. A few turned to crime. Comics shifted from being stories about cute little rascals to being dark dramas about gangster-fighting heroes such as Dick Tracy. Jerry told Joe that he wanted to create his own comic, about a special kind of crime-fighter.

The boys worked so hard on Jerry's project that they flunked their school year. This didn't stop them. They kept trying new heroes, new plots. "It took us six years to sell Superman," Jerry Siegel used to say. (Actually it was more like four years, but Jerry was a melodramatic storyteller.) Sometime in 1934 he came up with a script starring a broad-shouldered stranger from another planet who seemed like a nerd but had super-strength. Joe drew the new he-man throwing bad guys around like beach balls.

The boys sent their superhero comic strip off to all the pulp publishers they could think of. No one bothered to write back, but a few kept the proposal in their desk drawers. One was Charlie Gaines. A former school principal, he'd lost his job and was selling comic strips to newsstand distributors.

Two and a half years went by and still no one seemed to want Superman. The geeky boys from Cleveland went on living with their mothers, and sending obscure magazines other strips about characters such as a Chinese villain called Fui Onyui (these were casually racist times). Then it happened: Someone in Charlie Gaines's office saw an outline of their Superman idea, and wrote to see if the boys would like to contribute a Superman story for a new magazine to be called *Action Comics*. The boys said yes, and worked frantically over weekends and late into the night to produce a strip.

The people who bought *Action Comics* No. 1 liked Superman a lot. They went back to their newsstands to place their orders for the next edition. Charlie Gaines reported this reader interest to the publisher, Harold Donenfeld, a hustler with connections to the underworld and a background in publishing magazines with half-naked women on the covers. Gaines and his boss, Donenfeld, put Superman into more editions of *Action*. By *Action Comics'* issue No. 5, readers were embracing the Man of Steel.

By now, Europe was on the brink of war with Germany. The Americans were also feeling anxious – and what was more cheering than reading stories about a super-strong man on their side? Like so many Americans, Superman was an immigrant, someone who'd come from a world to which he could never return. He was an outsider always trying to fit in. People at his work even made fun of him. But he could burst out of the humiliation of daily life in a blaze of red-caped glory!

In 1938, Harry Donenfeld summoned the boys to Action Comics' New York office to discuss a contract. Joe and Jerry, no doubt congratulating themselves on their own genius, took the train to New York City and signed a ten-year deal to produce so many pages a month in exchange for a salary and a share of the net profits.

Donenfeld knew, and the boys did not know, that "net profits" means whatever is left over after the accountants finish paying all other expenses – left over, that is, after Harry, Charlie, and everyone else had taken their cut. In return, Action Comics gave Jerry and Joe a deal beyond their wildest dreams – at least until their dreams caught up with Superman's success. The boys hadn't realized that there might be huge profits from spinoffs; they had never thought about T-shirts and TV shows. Television had been invented by that time, but it wasn't something people had in their homes.

By 1939 Superman had his own magazine, which was selling 900,000 copies an issue. The next year *The Adventures of Superman* went on the radio. A comic strip about the Man of Steel was picked up by three hundred newspapers. By the end of 1941, with war raging, Superman was reaching about 35 million people, by either radio or print. And cigar-chomping Donenfeld was spending his share of the profits, millions of dollars, in the casinos of Cuba, with his mobster friends.

It was only a matter of time before the newspapers reported Donenfeld's criminal connections. Then they dug up the fact that Donenfeld had got his start in girlie magazines. The image of comics, never wholesome, now began to seem actually sinister. Meanwhile, parents and church leaders noticed that there were a lot of people flying around in their underwear in comic books, and a lot of violence – all in all, a bad influence on young readers. "Unless we want a coming generation even more ferocious than the present one," wrote a *Chicago Daily News* columnist in 1940, "parents and teachers throughout America must band together to break the 'comic' magazine." The *Daily News* estimated that it had 25 million requests for reprints of this article.

Over in England, the anti-Nazi writer George Orwell warned that Superman fans had much in common with the "bully-worship" that had brought Hitler and Mussolini to power. Yet Hitler and Mussolini weren't Superman fans either. *Das Schwarze Korps*, the magazine of Hitler's ruthless *Schutzstaffel* police, or SS, published an article describing Jerry Siegel as "intellectually and physically circumcised," and added that "American youth . . . don't even notice the poison they swallow" when they read Superman.

But everyone else loved comics, even soldiers in the U.S. army. Every month, readers pored over Superman and the other new superheroes –

Batman, Commando Yank, the Star-Spangled Kid, Captain America, and Wonder Woman – waging patriotic battles against villains with names like Baron Gestapo and Captain Nippon. Wrapped in the flag, the comic-book musclemen (and women) humiliated America's enemies.

The war ended in 1945. So did the golden age of superhero comics. Suddenly readers turned off, perhaps feeling that the superheroes' work was done. Instead of selling in the millions, an issue of *Superman* would sell a mere 700,000 copies. As the soldiers returned to ordinary civilian life, most of the comic strips, an estimated 90 percent, died off.

Comic-book publishers scrambled frantically to figure out what to try next. Some had already shifted during the war to heavy crime comics such as *Crime Does Not Pay* (a particularly violent strip whose cover once featured Lucky Luciano, one of Harry Donenfeld's real-life mobster pals). By 1947, *Crime Does Not Pay* was outselling Captain Marvel and Superman. True-love comics were another new direction; by 1949 there were more than a hundred of them.

Charlie Gaines, the former high-school principal, thought he knew what readers wanted. He started a company named Education Comics, which put out *Picture Stories from the Bible* and *Picture Stories from American History*. But word came back from the magazine sellers that kids were trading ten Education Comics for one issue of *Batman*. In 1947, while Charlie was roaring around a lake in his new powerboat, he crashed the boat and died. His son William inherited the company, and discovered that it was $100,000 in debt.

Bill Gaines changed the company's name to Entertaining Comics, and tried out new titles – *Crypt of Terror* and *Vault of Horror*. After the real horrors of the war, people were ready for melodramatic, make-believe horror that made them laugh. Young Bill and his team of writers tried to outdo each other with sick humor. In one story, a man wanders into a restaurant and discovers that it is run by vampires, with a menu offering French-fried scabs and blood cocktails. These comics were gross, but they grabbed readers.

Not everyone was amused. Fredric Wertham had emigrated from Germany in the 1920s to work in New York as a psychologist specializing in troubled kids. A kind man but a snob, he didn't think much of American culture from the start. When he noticed that many juvenile delinquents read comic books, instead of concluding that maybe ten-cent comics were all the kids could afford, he began to write articles claiming that comic books were pushing modern American youth into juvenile delinquency.

In conferences and magazines, Wertham kept up his attack. In his eyes, even the Man of Steel was disgusting – in fact, he was a closet Nazi. "Superman (with the big S on his uniform – we should, I suppose, be thankful it is not an SS) needs an endless stream of ever new sub-men, criminals and foreign-looking people," he wrote. "Superman has long been recognized as a symbol of violent race superiority. . . . [He] explicitly belongs to a super race."

Wertham's claim drove the folks in the comic-publishing industry crazy. From Donenfeld down to Joe and Jerry they were mostly Jewish, and here was some guy with a German accent telling them that their hero was

Fredric Wertham, testifying before a United States congressional committee in May 1954. Not only did he believe that comics could lead to juvenile crime, he predicted that adults would never find any value in them. Wrong on both counts; some vintage comics now sell for hundreds of dollars.

YOU CAN'T READ THIS

Hitler's stooge. Worse yet, Wertham's anti-comic campaigns were having an effect.

In 1948 the city of Los Angeles announced that there would be a $500 fine or six months in jail as penalty for selling crime comics to kids under eighteen. In 1951 Canada passed a law against importing U.S. crime comics. New York City cops seized thousands of copies right off newsstands. The U.S. National Congress of Parents and Teachers came up with a "plan of action" against "unwholesome" graphic magazines. People in Massachusetts piled comic books on bonfires and cheered as the pages went up in smoke.

Meanwhile, there was trouble right inside Donenfeld's company. After signing that ten-year contract in 1938, Joe and Jerry had watched as millions of dollars in profits went to the publishers. They felt they had been ripped off. They now had families to support. Joe, who had always been near-sighted, was going blind. But the contract was coming up for renewal. Though sales of comics were down, the *Superman* radio show was still going strong, and Donenfeld had been talking to Hollywood film producers about a movie. Superman's inventors wanted their share of the super-profits.

They launched a lawsuit for $5 million and the return of all *Superman* rights. But they were no match for Donenfeld. They had to settle not for $5 million but for $100,000 – and they owed most of that to their lawyer.

Joe and Jerry were shocked. Superman, their creation, was now other people's property. The two friends lost their moment at the top. Jerry wrote for *Superman* for a while but other people were his bosses. The team of Siegel and Shuster was finished, though the two stayed friends for life.

Meanwhile, over at the Entertaining Comics group, Charlie Gaines's son Bill and his team were gleefully pushing deeper into the territory of bad taste. One early 1950s EC comic, *Crime SuspenStories*, featured a cover showing an axe murderer, hatchet still dripping, standing over a headless woman's body. Gaines thought that one was so outrageous it was funny.

Fredric Wertham did not. This particular issue became one of his major pieces of evidence in his crusade against comics. He used it in his book *Seduction of the Innocent*, published in 1954. Things came to a head in May of that year. The U.S. Senate decided to hold a special session on links between mobsters and the comics industry. Bill Gaines and Fredric Wertham were called to testify. Would this be a clash of the titans?

Wertham spoke to the Senate hearings first. He told chilling case histories of psychopaths who loved horror fantasy. He misquoted comic-book plots and zeroed in on some of the insults the characters threw at one another. When it came to teaching violence and race hatred, he declared, "Hitler was a beginner compared to the comic-book industry."

Then it was Bill Gaines's turn to speak. He was a chubby man, and had been taking pills to lose weight. They made him dozy just when he needed his wits about him. As the senators lobbed questions at him, he felt himself fading away. He actually mumbled that he considered the headless corpse on the cover of *Crime SuspenStories* in "good taste – for a horror comic." Before he left the room, Gaines knew he had been a disaster. He went home and took to his bed for three days.

In the end, the Senate decided that it couldn't do much about comics without infringing on constitutional principles of free speech. It agreed to stop short of banning comic books after the industry agreed to police itself by adopting a new Comics Code. The Code promised that there would be no more bloody axes, no more offensive slang, no more showing policemen or judges in ways that invited disrespect. The Code even asked comics to drop the word "weird." Without weirdness the fun was gone, so Bill Gaines closed down EC's comics business. In rebellion, he and his pals invented *Mad Magazine*, which was both gross and goofy. *Mad* got him into trouble too – but because *Mad* was a magazine, it was outside the Comics Code.

As for Fredric Wertham, for a generation comics fans hated his name. They cursed him as the man who had killed off some of the world's wildest flights of imagination. Thanks to him, Superman and Batman were like lonely war veterans in a wholesome world of Archie and Daffy Duck.

In his old age, Fredric Wertham had a change of heart. In 1974, in his last book, *The World of Fanzines: A Special Form of Communication*, he explained that comic-book fans were very nice kids after all. This book didn't sell nearly as well as his earlier hysterical, scare-mongering shockers.

But then, horror and fantasy are much more fun to read than simple common sense. Wertham should have learned that much, at least, from the writers he had attacked.

Days of the Taliban

DURING LONG PERIODS of violence and war, when those in authority want to bring their chaotic world under control, often they start by trying to control reading.

It is late September 2001, and the summer heat still bakes the streets of Kabul, Afghanistan. Nelofer Ayub is stifling inside her burqa, the pale blue robe that covers her from head to foot. The burqa's only opening is a cloth cage, a sort of netting, around her eyes. The sixteen-year-old has been wearing a burqa since the Taliban took over Kabul more than five years ago – that is, all her teenaged life. It's hard for her to see her feet – or anything except what's directly in front. As she walks she's afraid she will trip, so she concentrates on staying close to her brother, Ahmed. This burqa smells like a sweaty tent, but Nelofer doesn't dare flap the cloth to let in more air. She cannot draw attention to herself. Afghanistan's rulers, a gang of black-turbaned men (they call themselves Taliban, "religious students"), have passed laws saying that females may not go out unless accompanied by a male relative. The Taliban have also decreed that girls may not attend school.

And Nelofer is on her way to a secret school, to break that law.

After the fall of the Taliban regime in Afghanistan in 2002, girls were allowed into classrooms again. But many girls in developing countries still lack the money or opportunity to go to school. It's estimated that of the world's 120 million children who cannot go to school, two-thirds are girls.

If one of the Taliban stops her on the street and discovers what she's up to, she knows, she will be beaten – or worse. The Taliban, with their whips and clubs, enforce an extreme form of Islam, one that insists that women be kept veiled in public and always obey the wishes of their menfolk. According to the Taliban way of thinking, if females want to learn to read, it is a sure sign that they are not religious. As for females who can already read, the Taliban assume that they must have been taught by the communists who used to rule Afghanistan.

Nelofer can remember the early 1990s, when the Afghan communists and their Soviet Russian protectors ran this part of her country. People complained, and some openly loathed the communists. But she can also remember that girls went to school in those days, and that women, tens of thousands of Kabul women wearing Western clothes, their faces bare, went off to work in offices and as doctors and lawyers and teachers. It's hard to believe that, back then, her parents and their friends dreamed of getting rid of the Soviet-backed communists, and spoke about how the city would be liberated by religious warriors from the wild countryside.

In 1992 the Russian Soviets abandoned Afghanistan, leaving the local communists to fight alone. Civil war between different Afghan factions got bloodier; the noise of gunfire got closer and closer. Gradually, thanks to money and support from Pakistan, the United States, and rich Saudi Arabians like Osama bin Laden, the Taliban emerged as the one group that could beat the others. Their leader was one of Osama's sons-in-law, a rough, heavily bearded, one-eyed warrior named Mullah Omar. It was said that the only book he had ever read was the Koran, the holy book of Islam. It was said that he was proud to be ignorant – he thought it meant he was simple and pure of heart.

Nelofer also remembers 1996, when the Taliban swept into Kabul. "All sisters who are working in government offices are hereby informed to stay home until further notice," the radio announced, the day after the Taliban's white flag went up over the city. "All sisters are seriously asked to cover their faces and the whole of their bodies when they go out." At the University of Kabul, eight thousand female undergraduate students learned that their education had come to a sudden end. Any female who showed her face or showed that she could read was assumed to be a communist, and the Taliban's enemy.

Nelofer and her brother, Ahmed, are not communists. Their father has a small business importing goods. (Under the Taliban's strict religious rules, this sometimes gets him into trouble – like the time he brought in cases of shampoo with a picture of a pretty woman's face on the label. Angry young men in black turbans, who call themselves religious police, made her father and his workers scribble out the faces on the labels with felt-tipped pens. They said it was against the law of God to show images of a woman's face.) As for Nelofer's mother, who used to teach grade one, the Taliban told her she couldn't work at all. Since they took over, she has sat at home, feeling sick and depressed.

And Mother, still having a husband, is one of the lucky ones! It's estimated that there are fifty thousand widows in Kabul, women whose husbands died in the civil wars. Since women can now only go out in public with a male from their family, many widows have to stay in their houses – or risk being whipped by the religious police.

Nelofer can imagine how terrible it must be for a mother to hear her child clamoring for food or a chance to play in the park, and to know she doesn't dare go out the front door. Occasionally Nelofer sees women begging for bread. But not all the beggars in burqas are helpless; some are spies. They could be watching today – now – as Nelofer and her brother go into this battered apartment building and mount the stairs to the one place where Nelofer can let her mind out of its cage.

For one of these apartments is a secret school. The girls come at different times, by different routes and on different days each week, to disguise their activities. The woman who runs the school, Mrs. Fazel, is taking a huge risk by teaching her five students. She believes that teaching children is not a sin, but the moral thing to do.

Nelofer enters the apartment, two almost bare rooms whose windows are covered in paint. (The Taliban ordered all windows painted so no one could see women inside their homes.) The only furniture is a cupboard full of pieces of cloth and boxes of needles and thread. If the religious police do burst through the door, the girls will appear to be sewing clothes – one of the few activities women are allowed to do.

Nelofer's cousin Feroza used to attend a mosque school near the city of Ghazni, run by a religious teacher. "From eight a.m. until four p.m., we sat on the floor – there were no chairs – and we learned Arabic so we could read the Koran," Feroza told Nelofer once. "He never taught us what we were reading. We could read the sounds, that's all." When Feroza turned ten, the religious teacher kicked her out of school. "He said I should not study any more. He said, if girls study, they become witches." After that, a friend of the family came to visit her parents once a month to teach her and her cousins to read Pashto and Dari, the languages of Afghanistan. He brought simple books, and taught history, geography, and mathematics.

All across Afghanistan, girls have found ways to study in secret. One United Nations official estimates that more than twenty-five thousand girls and women across Herat province alone have been able to find some kind of lessons, right under the Taliban's noses. But secret schools have almost no books. The Taliban have banned all books with pictures, and all books from Europe, America, or countries (such as Iran) that practice Shia Islam, a different form of the religion. When the Taliban find private libraries in people's houses, they dump the books in trucks and cart them away to be burned in huge public bonfires.

Once Mrs. Fazel's apartment had a bookshelf of books in Persian, Arabic, and English. All you can see on the shelves now is those heaps of sewing. But beneath the piles of sewing are stapled photocopies – home-made, illegal, dangerous books.

They don't look like much, these books, but they are the delight of Nelofer's life. They tell the girls about history – real history, not communist or Taliban propaganda. They tell of a wide and wonder-filled world beyond the girls' burqa cages. They tell of such people as En-hedu-anna, the high priestess of Ur, who wrote poems to a goddess of love and war more than four thousand years ago. They tell of Alexander the Great, who came through Afghanistan with his Greek soldiers (and his beloved copies of Homer) over two thousand years ago, and named a city Alexandria-in-Arachosia – now it's called Kandahar. After the Greeks came the Mongols, and then, in the 1800s, the British tried to control this country, and after them, the Russians. Sooner or later, the Afghans drove them all out.

Nelofer's favorite history lesson was the day Mrs. Fazel told the girls about a remarkable woman from the 1400s. Her name was Queen Gower Shad, her husband was a descendant of Genghis Khan, and she ruled until she was in her eighties. Her empire stretched almost from China to

Turkey. Queen Gower Shad built fine libraries and religious colleges covered in delicately painted tiles the color of the bluest skies. Travelers said her libraries were among the most beautiful buildings in the world.

When Nelofer reads about women like Gower Shad, she looks around her so-called school with its painted-over windows and anxious students, and she wonders how her country has come to this – from being enriched by great civilizations, to living under the Taliban's cult of ignorance and cruel oppression. What would Queen Gower Shad make of this?

Afghan girls are no longer afraid to be photographed. Some have faces that reveal their Mongol ancestors; others, with fair hair and light eyes, may be descended from the Greeks who invaded the region under Alexander the Great.

She also reads that Gower Shad was the patron of a great poet, Hakim Jami, who studied Plato and other Greek philosophers, and wrote some of the loveliest poems in classical Persian. One of Nelofer's favorite passages includes the lines "It is in the nature of Beauty to reveal herself, and to remain morose behind a veil; For Beauty does not tolerate being hidden and, if imprisoned, will peep through the window of her cell. . . ."

Jami's poem comforts Nelofer when, at the end of class, she has to put her smelly burqa back over her head. As she creeps carefully downstairs to meet Ahmed, watching warily through her cloth cage, she tells herself, "If imprisoned, Beauty will peep through the window of her cell."

Ahmed is in a strange mood when he meets her outside the apartment building. He too has been doing something forbidden – listening to the BBC World Service, British radio news. He speaks in a low but excited voice. "On September 11, some men hijacked airplanes and flew them into skyscrapers in New York City," he says. "The buildings came crashing down. Thousands of people were killed." There's more; the radio says the Americans think these terrorists were working for Osama bin Laden – the man behind the Taliban – who now lives here in Afghanistan, near his son-in-law, the Taliban leader, Mullah Omar. Maybe the Americans will attack Afghanistan, says Ahmed. Maybe there will be another war. "Maybe," he whispers, "maybe they will drive out the Taliban."

Nelofer is shocked. She hates the thought of another wave of outsiders barging into her country, and she is alarmed by the prospect of more blood-shed, more destruction. But for the first time in a long while, she wonders if she can see a future without a burqa – without the cage that has confined her for the past five years. She wonders if she can see a future in a bigger, wider world – the one she knows only through her reading.

18

Access Denied

CODES AND CODE-BREAKING *techniques have come a long way since the time of Mary, Queen of Scots. After some inventors came up with machines that could create hugely complicated codes, other inventors developed machines that could crack the codes. These so-called computers evolved into the supercomputers that generate today's so-far unbreakable military ciphers. Have we finally found a way to block people from reading what we don't want them to read?*

ou know this scene from a spy movie or a science-fiction thriller: The hero sits down in front of a computer to check out a vital clue, to unmask a treacherous villain. Suddenly, up pops a chilling message: ACCESS DENIED. With a shock, the hero realizes that all that desperately needed information is locked up behind an electronic wall. The machine has said, *You can't read this.*

For thousands of years, people have been creating devices to prevent other people from reading texts they want to keep secret. The ancient Greeks of Sparta used a coding tool called a skytale (ski-ta-le) to send secret messages in times of battle. The skytale consisted of a wooden stick and a strip of leather wound round it like the stripes on a candy cane. Soldiers would write their messages on the strip along the length of the stick, and then unwind the strip. That broke up the pattern of the message, separating the words and making them meaningless – until the strip was delivered to some other Spartan who wound it around a stick of the same thickness, restoring the words to a meaningful pattern.

All messages are patterns of meaning, and recognizing something about their pattern is the key to breaking a code. More than a thousand years ago Arab cryptanalysts (*kryptos* is Greek for "secret") understood that in any language, certain letters and common words appear frequently; they used "frequency analysis" to break codes by recognizing their most frequently occurring parts.

Around 1460, a very clever Italian inventor named Leon Alberti (he was also the author of the first major book on architectural design) came up with a plan for a coding machine: alphabets on movable disks. Through a simple turn of the disks, ABCDEFG on disk 1 might line up with PQRSTUV on disk 2 and HIJKLMN on disk 3. If you wanted to code the message BAD FEED (warning your friends not to feed their horses), you would substitute for B the letter Q from disk 2 and for A the letter H from disk 3, and then go back to disk 2 for the "D." The entire message would read QHS MTLS. Alberti's double substitution system meant that frequency analysis (the strategy that cracked Mary, Queen of Scots' code) would be difficult, because common letters like E or A would be written in more than one way.

In the time of Frederick Douglass, Confederate officers in the American Civil War carried versions of Alberti's code disk. But not until World War I did people develop a seriously complicated version. On August 26, 1914, a German cruiser ran aground on the shores of the Baltic Sea, and the Russians seized German navy codes. They shared this information with the English, and it gave them the power to decode many German messages right through to the end of the war. In the mid-1920s the German military command learned that their enemies had been decoding their messages, and realized that they had to come up with a better coding system, a better machine – one so complex that no human analyst could possibly beat it.

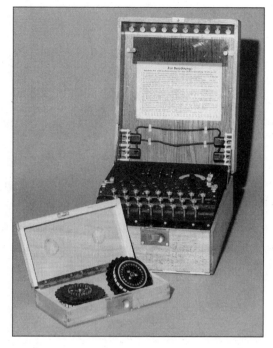

The Enigma cipher machine created new codes each day for military messages, yet it could fit neatly into a wooden carrying case. The Nazis were convinced that Enigma's codes were unbreakable.

A German inventor, Arthur Scherbius, had already produced just such a machine: the Enigma, a fearsome thing that looked like a typewriter with a box on top. Inside were scrambler disks that rotated each time one of the alphabet's twenty-six letters was typed in. In his first version, Scherbius put in three scrambler disks, which meant there were 26 x 26 x 26 = 17,576 possible settings. To unscramble a message coded by an Enigma machine, you needed to know the day's settings – for example, that today disk 1 was rotated so that W was at the top (and the alphabet started from there), and that today disk 2 had C at the top and disk 3 had Q at the top. If you set your own Enigma to the same "WCQ" key and typed in the scrambled version, out would come the decoded message. But anyone without that day key would have to spend days trying possible versions – and by that time there would have been several new keys.

Scherbius died in 1929, but his Enigma kept evolving. For later models the designers added more disks, and other refinements that swapped the letters around even more. With 1,305,093,289,500 possible combinations, the Enigma seemed to Germany's top officers to be invincible. They ordered thirty thousand of the machines as they prepared to march across Europe and into World War II.

But they hadn't counted on two brilliant mathematicians: a slim Polish man in glasses, Marian Rejewski, and a shaggy Englishman, Alan Turing. These two nerds didn't carry guns or fly bomber planes, but they played a crucial role in the defeat of Enigma and, ultimately, the Nazis.

Rejewski's breakthrough came first. In the 1930s, working for the Polish Cipher Bureau, he noticed that the Germans put the day key (in code, mind you) at the top of the first messages of the day. He also noticed other patterns in Enigma's chains of letters, and realized they were the unique products of the day's settings for the scramblers. So he catalogued all the possible scrambler settings. The job took many months, but eventually allowed him to look up the patterns and identify likely scrambler settings.

Then, around 1938, the Enigma designers suddenly increased the number of scrambler disks, raising the number of possible combinations into the millions of trillions. The Poles knew that their country was in danger, and that decoding would now require more resources than they had at their disposal. They took their replicas of Enigma machines and smuggled them to England. Just in time; in September 1939, Nazi tanks rolled into Poland. Marian Rejewski escaped through Romania, to France and then to England. The war had begun.

The English, meanwhile, had set up a top-secret decoding headquarters in Bletchley Park, a manor house deep in the green English countryside. There they assembled a strange assortment of brainy men and women: mathematicians, people who studied languages, all the British chess grandmasters, people who were very fast at solving crossword puzzles. Perhaps because Rejewski was from a country now occupied by Germans, the British did not trust him enough to invite him to Bletchley. The brilliant cryptographer was in effect denied access, and spent the war working at a low-level job in London.

Luckily for the English, they had their own mathematicians, many of them from Cambridge University. One was Alan Turing. In the 1930s, while Rejewski was breaking the early Enigma codes, Turing had been writing his PhD thesis on machines that could theoretically be designed to carry out problems in logic, such as recognizing patterns among "computable numbers" or, for that matter, chess moves – or coded messages. The British government assigned Turing to design a version of this machine for Bletchley Park.

Even among Bletchley's mad scientists, Turing stood out: messy and absent-minded, he had a high, shrill laugh. He loved Disney's movie *Snow White and the Seven Dwarves*. Sometimes, when he bicycled to work at the manor house, he wore a gas mask because of his hay fever. But his "Turing machines," or "bombes" – walls of clattering wheels that scanned spinning tape – did the trick. Like an electronic version of Rejewski's catalogues, they could check out twenty possible Enigma settings per second. On good days, the Bletchley team would figure out the day key within an hour of receiving the first intercepted German message.

By the middle of the war, the British were reading most German communications: which ships the submarines were going to attack, what troops were moving where. One British commander estimated that without the work at Bletchley Park, the war in Europe would have dragged on until 1948, instead of ending in 1945.

But the end of the war only brought increasing suspicion and fear between Communist countries and Western countries. Then, in 1949, Soviet Russia exploded an atomic bomb. The West was horrified that this potential enemy had grown so dangerous, and the international mood of suspicion turned into the bristling hostility of the Cold War.

Although the first true American computer, the Electronic Numerical Integrator And Calculator, or ENIAC, wasn't finished until 1945, the United States had emerged from the war as the most powerful and richest nation on Earth. It had taken over as world leader in developing computers – and in deciding who would work on them. In 1951 several Cambridge

University men who had worked for British intelligence in the war were unmasked as Soviet spies. Turing had never been a spy, but he had gone to Cambridge. He had the wrong friends. In 1952 word got out that he was homosexual, and under the laws of the time this made him a criminal. He was humiliated – but worse was to come. He was told he could no longer work on secret decoding projects.

Alan Turing committed suicide in 1954. He did it by eating a poisoned apple – an idea he took from the movie *Snow White*. But his electronic brainchildren, the machines that could think, kept growing and changing.

Financed largely by the U.S. Defense Department, computer designers began to develop machines that could not only solve problems but could "talk" to each other in a network. The Defense Department set up the Advanced Research Projects Agency (ARPA), which by 1969 brought

Though he became famous as a brilliant mathematician, Alan Mathison Turing had a rocky time at school, where he floundered in English and was criticized by his teachers for handing in messy assignments. Still, he won most of his school's math prizes.

on line a network of computers from the military world, big business, universities, and libraries, all sharing information. The designers deliberately made this system as decentralized as possible, with all kinds of electronic pathways, so that if one part of the net was attacked, the computers could keep sharing information by other routes. In those days this network was known as the ARPANet. Today we call it the Internet, and it is as close as humankind has yet come to a giant public library, a vast treasure trove of reading.

Of course, there are times when computer information is not accessible. You can lose your password. You can be denied access to Internet sites. People who disagree with governments in China or Saudi Arabia are used to seeing messages on their screens like "Server down" or "Website not found."

But when people really want to read something, they can be patient and systematic, like Marian Rejewski and Alan Turing. They try different routes, different patterns, different passwords. They know that, given the power of human curiosity, the breadth of human ingenuity, and the power of human resolve, it has been pointless, so far, to tell people, "You can't read this."

Source Notes

Introduction

A version of the story of Tarquin and the Sibyl can be found in *A History of Reading*, by Alberto Manguel (Alfred A. Knopf, 1996). The story of the Sorcerer's Apprentice can be seen in the film *Fantasia* (Disney Studios, 1940). A version of it is told in *Folklore and Book Culture*, by Kevin Hayes (University of Tennessee Press, 1997).

1: *The First Readers*

For life in Ur see *Everyday Life in Ancient Mesopotamia*, by Jean Bottero (Johns Hopkins University Press, 2001), and *Sumer and the Sumerians*, by Harriet Crawford (Cambridge University Press, 1991). For En-hedu-anna see *A Book of Women Poets from Antiquity to Now*, by Aliki Barnstone and Willis Barnstone (Schocken Books, 1992), *A History of Reading*, by Stephen Fischer (Reaktion Books, 2003), and *A History of Reading*, by Manguel. My version of her hymn is adapted from *The Electronic Text Corpus of Sumerian Literature*, by J.A. Black, G. Cunningham, E. Robson, and G. Zolyomi (Oxford, 1998).

2: *Language Lost and Language Found*

For the story of Arthur Evans see *The Find of a Lifetime*, by Sylvia Horwitz (Weidenfeld and Nicolson, 1981), and *Minotaur: Sir Arthur Evans and the Archaeology of the Minoan Myth* (Hill and Wang, 2000), by J. Alexander MacGillivray. The above books touch on Michael Ventris's work. For a fuller description see *The Code Book: The Evolution of Secrecy from Mary, Queen of Scots to Quantum Cryptography*, by Simon Singh (Doubleday, 1999).

3: The Poet and the Emperor

A good biography is *Nero*, by Richard Holland (Sutton, 2000). For the story of Lucan see chapter 9 in *Ambitiosa Mors: Suicide and Self in Roman Thought and Literature*, by Timothy Hill (Routledge, 2004), and the General Introduction of *Lucan: Pharsalia*, translated and edited by Jane Wilson Joyce (Cornell University Press, 1993).

4: The Made-to-Order Alphabet

The name of the monk Gorioun is sometimes spelled Koriun or Koryun. The name of Mesrob is sometimes spelled Mesrop. For Mesrob's story see *The Armenian People from Ancient Times to Modern*, Vol. I, by Richard Hovanissian (St. Martin's Press, 1997), and *Mesrop Mashtots*, by E.B. Aghayan (Yerevan University Press, 1986); the quote about Mesrob's vision is on page 37 of the latter, attributed to the monk Moses Khorenatsi. For background on Edessa see *From the Holy Mountain*, by William Dalrymple (HarperCollins, 1997). Thanks to Professor Ed Safarian for the anecdote about his son, the artist Paul Safarian.

5: The Prayerful Pagodas

For more about Shotoku (also known as Koken) see *The Chrysanthemum Throne: A History of Emperors of Japan*, by Peter Martin (Sutton, 1997). For more on the *darani* project see *The History of Japanese Printing and Book Illustration*, by David Chibbett (Kodansha International, 1977), and *A History of Reading*, by Fischer.

6: The Stolen Story

The incident of the Genji manuscript theft can be found in *Murasaki Shikibu: Her Diary and Poetic Memoirs: A Translation and Study*, by Richard Bowring (Princeton University Press, 1982). See also *A Woman's Weapon: Spirit Possession in The Tale of Genji*, by Doris Bargen (University of Hawaii Press, 1997), and *The Force of Women in Japanese History*, by Mary Beard (Foreign Affairs Press, 1953). A fictionalized version of Lady Murasaki's life (and the incident of the manuscript theft) can be found in *The Tale of Murasaki*, by Liza Dalby (Nan Talese, Random House, 2000).

7: The Pillage of Baghdad

The descriptions of Baghdad before and after Hulagu, and the quoted description from Anwari, come from The Story of Civilization: Vol IV, *The Age of Faith*, by Will and Ariel Durant (Simon & Schuster, 1950). The quote "Hardly ever has Islam . . ." is from *Early Mongol Rule in 13th Century Iran: A Persian Renaissance*, by George Lane (Routledge, Curzon, 2003). A good account of Genghis Khan and his grandsons appears in *The Mongol Warlords*, by David Nicolle (G.E. Lane, 1990). Details about the pillage of the great library in Alexandria and the destruction of Baghdad's libraries come from A *History of Libraries in the Western World*, by Michael D. Harris (Scarecrow Press, 1999).

8: Giving Books to the People

Sejong is sometimes spelled Seijong. Hangul is sometimes spelled Hankul. Confucius is sometimes spelled K'ung-fu-tzu. For the story of young Sejong see *King Seijong The Great*, by Chan Cho Hyon Pae (King Seijong Memorial Society, 1970), and A *History of Korea*, by Roger Tennant (Kegan Paul, 1996). For Confucian opposition to Hangul see A *Sourcebook of Korean Civilization*, by Peter Lee (Columbia University Press, 1993). For Sejong's motivations in creating Hangul see *King Sejong the Great: The Light of 15th-century Korea*, edited by Young-Key Kim Renaud (George Washington University Press, 1992). For Gutenberg see *The Gutenberg Revolution*, by John Man (Headline Publishing, Hodder Headline, 2002), and *Gutenberg: Man of the Millennium*, by a writing team headed by Peter Krawietz (Verlag Hermann Schmidt, Mainz, 2000).

9: Darkness upon the Deep

For details about Luther's books, Peter Schoeffer's meeting with Tyndale, book smuggling, and Tyndale's comments on Hebrew, see *God's Bestseller: William Tyndale, Thomas More, and the Writing of the English Bible – A Story of Martyrdom and Betrayal*, by Brian Moynahan (St. Martin's Press, 2002). For Cochlaeus's encounter with Tyndale's publishing venture, Anne Boleyn's interest in Tyndale, and Phillips's betrayal of Tyndale, see *William Tyndale*, by C.H. Williams (Thomas Nelson and Sons, 1969). For Tyndale's contribution to the English language see A *History of Reading*, by Manguel.

10: *The Cousins and the Code*

For a good retelling of Claude Nau and the messages smuggled in beer barrels see *Mary Queen of Scots*, by Antonia Fraser (Weidenfeld & Nicolson, 1969). For Tom Phelippes's forgery and code-cracking see also *The Code Book*, by Singh.

11: *Books Not to be Read*

For stories of Eirikur, Bogi, Magnus, and the Black School, see *Folklore and Book Culture*, by Hayes. For the *Index Librorum Prohibitorum* see *100 Banned Books: Censorship Histories of World Literature*, by Nicholas Karolides, Margaret Bald, and Dawn B. Sova (Checkmate Books/Facts on File, 1999). For the censoring of Albertus Magnus and Harry Potter see *Nihil Obstat: Catalogue for an exhibition of banned, censored and challenged books in the West, 1491–2000*, by Pearce J. Carefoote, introduction by Alberto Manguel (Thomas Fisher Rare Book Library, University of Toronto, 2005).

12: *That Dreadful Mr. Shakespeare*

For Newbery's bookshop and the world of early children's books (including Anna Laetitia Barbauld), and for the lives of Charles and Mary Lamb, see *Mad Mary Lamb*, by Susan Tyler Hitchcock (W.W. Norton and Co., 2005). For the Bowdlers see *Dr. Bowdler's Legacy: A History of Expurgated Books in England and America*, by Noel Perrin (Atheneum, 1969). For Thomas Bowdler's writings in *The British Critic* and Harriet Bowdler's *Sermons on the Doctrines and Duties of Christianity* see the British Library in London (not many people read Harriet these days – the pages of the edition I read were uncut, which means I was the first person in more than 150 years to read them!)

13: *A Book at His Fingertips*

For the story of Louis Braille's childhood and family life see *Louis Braille*, by Beverley Birch (Gareth Stevens Children's Books, 1989). For Braille's education see also *The Life and Work of Louis Braille 1809–1852*, by Pierre Henri (South African National Council for the Blind, 1987). For the fate of Braille's hands and the state of Braille today I am indebted to Darleen Bogart, past president of the International Council of English Braille, and also to the Canadian National Institute for the Blind.

14: *Freddy the Slave Boy*

For the early life of Frederick Douglass and how he learned to read see *My Bondage and My Freedom, Part I*, by Frederick Douglass (Miller, Orton and Mulligan, 1855), and *Young Frederick Douglass*, by Dickson J. Preston (Johns Hopkins University Press, 1980). For laws against slaves learning to read see *When I Can Read My Title Clear: Literacy, Slavery and Religion in the Antebellum South*, by Janet Duitsman Cornelius (University of South Carolina Press, 1991). For Douglass's name change, comments on his career as an orator, his statement at Seneca Falls, and his support for women's suffrage, see *Frederick Douglass and the Fight for Freedom*, by Douglas T. Miller (Facts on File Publications, 1988).

15: *The Two-Faced Treaty*

For a good discussion of differing concepts in the Maori and English versions of the treaty see *The Illustrated History of the Treaty of Waitangi*, by Claudia Orange (Bridget Williams Books, 2004). This book is also very good for details about the celebrations and subsequent problems over land sales, fishing and mining rights, etc. For details of Hone Heke's acts of rebellion, John Somes's quote, and the Northern War, see *The Maori and the Crown*, by Dora Alves (Greenwood Press, 1999). For the evolution of the treaty from the nineteenth century until the end of the twentieth see *Trick or Treaty?: The Treaty of Waitangi*, by Douglas Graham (Institute for Policy Studies, New Zealand, 1997).

16: *The Evil World of – Comic Books?*

For the early days of Jerry Siegel and Joe Shuster, and for the best overview of the industry, see *Men of Tomorrow: Geeks, Gangsters and the Birth of the Comic Book*, by Gerard Jones (Basic Books, 2004). For more on Fredric Wertham see *Seal of Approval: The History of the Comics Code*, by Amy Kiste Nyberg (University Press of Mississippi, 1998). For Hitler's hatred of Superman see "Flying Up and Flying Down: The Rise and Fall of the American Superhero," *Harper's Magazine*, August 2004. For the Depression and the rise of comic books see *Censure et Bande Dessinée Américaine*, by Marc Jetté (Roussan, 1997). For Bill Gaines versus Fredric Wertham, horror/vampire comics, and the birth of *Mad Magazine*, see *Completely Mad: A History of the Comic Book and Magazine*, by Maria Reidelbach (Little, Brown, 1991).

17: *Days of the Taliban*

For a history of late-twentieth-century Afghanistan, the rise of the Taliban, and details about the fall of Kabul, see *Ghost Wars: The Secret History of the CIA, Afghanistan and bin Laden, from the Soviet Invasion to September 10, 2001*, by Steve Coll (Penguin, 2004). For the story of Gower Shad (sometimes spelled Gohar Shad) see *The Road to Oxiana*, by Robert Byron (Macmillan, 1939). I have adapted a poem by Hakim Jami found in *A Golden Treasury of Persian Poetry*, translated by Hadi Hassan (Indian Council for Cultural Relations, 1966). For details about girls learning to read under the Taliban, see *The Sewing Circles of Herat: A Personal Voyage through Afghanistan*, by Christina Lamb (HarperCollins, 2002), and Sally Armstrong's *Chatelaine Magazine* articles ("First Class" and other reports on women in Afghanistan, in 2002 and 2003), and *Veiled Threat: The Hidden Power of the Women of Afghanistan*, by Sally Armstrong (Penguin, 2002). I am indebted to Sally Armstrong, Adeena Niazi, and Dr. Sima Samar for putting me in touch with Afghan women who wish to remain nameless and who told me their stories; Nelofer is a composite of several of them. See also the excellent children's novels on Afghanistan by Deborah Ellis, *The Breadwinner* (Groundwood, 2000) and *Parvana's Journey* (Groundwood, 2002).

18: *Access Denied*

One of the best books on Alan Turing and his work is *Alan Turing: The Enigma*, by Andrew Hodges (Burnett Books/Hutchison, 1983). And of course the classic is *The Code Book*, by Singh. *A History of Modern Computing*, by Paul Ceruzzi (MIT Press, 2003) concentrates on the American developments after World War II. A good book on how the government of China attempts to block the Internet is *You've Got Dissent! Chinese Dissident Use of the Internet and Beijing's Counter-Strategies*, by Michael Chase and James Mulvenon (RAND, 2002). And I am grateful to Professor Wesley Wark of the University of Toronto, though any errors in my explanation of cryptanalysis are mine, not his.

Picture Notes

Every effort has been made to secure permission to reproduce copyrighted material in this book. Should any error or omission have been made, please notify the publisher and the information will be corrected in future editions.

Page

vi: Thomas Rowlandson illustration for "The Bookseller" in William Combe, *Doctor Syntax, His Three Tours in Search of the Picturesque, of Consolation, of a Wife*. (London: Chatto & Windus, 1868).

ix: Thomas Rowlandson illustration for "The Doctor's Dream" in William Combe, *Doctor Syntax, His Three Tours in Search of the Picturesque, of Consolation, of a Wife*. (London: Chatto & Windus, 1868).

2: *The Sybil of Cumae* painting by Domenico Zampieri, photograph by Erich Lessing, ART214635, Art Resource, NY.

5: Limestone Disk of Enhaduanna (En-hedu-anna), University of Pennsylvania Museum (image # 139330).

11: Sir Arthur Evans photograph by Col. Raymond ffennell, Ashmolean Museum, Oxford.

14: Michael Ventris photograph by Tom Blau, Camera Press London.

19: Colossal head of Emperor Nero, Staatliche Antikensammlung, Munich, Germany, ART190987, Bildarchiv Preussischer Kulturbesitz / Art Resource, NY.

31: Entrance to the Kasuga Shrine at Nara and Group of Consecrated Maidens, image # 1253785, Asian and Middle Eastern Division, The New York Public Library, Astor, Lennox, and Tilden Foundations.

35: *The Tale of Genji* woodcut by seventeenth-century artist Yamamoto Shunsho.

41: The Caliph, al-Musta'sim, brought before Hulagu Khan. A miniature. Permission British Library, Shelfmark Or. 2780, f.89v.

46: Portrait of Johannes Gutenberg by Andre Thevet, 1584.

52: Wood engraving by Abraham von Werdt, 1676.

57: The Tyndale New Testament, 1534. F1827 The Thomas Fisher Rare Book Library, University of Toronto.

61: Tyndale execution from *Foxe's Book of Martyrs*. F2548 The Thomas Fisher Rare Book Library, University of Toronto.

63: Mary Queen of Scots. Frontispiece, Agnes Strickland (Ed.), *Letters of Mary Queen of Scots* (London: Henry Colburn, 1843).

65: Walsingham. Illustration, Arthur D. Innes, *Ten Tudor Statesmen* (London: Eveleigh Nash, 1906).

69: "The Enchanter Merlin." Howard Pyle (author and illustrator), *The Story of King Arthur and his Knights* (London: George Newnes Limited, 1903). The Osborne Collection, Toronto Public Library.

71: Title page, *Index Librorum Prohibitorum*. F2546 The Thomas Fisher Rare Book Library, University of Toronto.

74: Francis Stephen Cary, portrait of Mary Lamb. NPG 1019 National Portrait Gallery, London.

77: Title page, Thomas Bowdler, *The Family Shakspeare*. F2549 The Thomas Fisher Rare Book Library, University of Toronto.

82: Portrait of Louis Braille, ART187603, Snark / Art Resource, NY.

92: Douglass. Frontispiece, Frederick Douglass, *My Bondage and My Freedom* (New York and Auburn: Miller, Orton & Mulligan, 1855).

95: Joseph Jenner Merrett, "The Warrior Chieftans of New Zealand. Harriet, Heke's wife; Heke; Kawiti." C-010-013 Alexander Turnbull Library, National Library of New Zealand.

97: Marcus King, "The Signing of the Treaty of Waitangi, Feb 6, 1840." C-033-007 Alexander Turnbull Library, National Library of New Zealand.

100: John Alexander Gilfillan, "Hone Heke," A-114-003 Alexander Turnbull Library, National Library of New Zealand.

102: Peter Hawkins (text) and Michael Dixon (illustrations), *The Halifax Explosion* (Toronto: True North Comics, 1997). By permission of McClelland & Stewart Ltd.

108: Photograph of Fredric Wertham by Gordon Parks, *New York World Telegram* (April 1954). LC-USZ62-135434 Library of Congress.

113 and 117: Photographs of schoolgirls in Afghanistan courtesy of Sally Armstrong.

121: "Enigma," Negative number MH2 7178, by permission of *The Trustees of the Imperial War Museum*, London.

124: Photograph of Alan Turing by Elliott & Fry. NPG x82217 National Portrait Gallery, London.

Acknowledgments

I'd like to thank the friends who read my manuscript and gave helpful suggestions, particularly Maria Kasstan and Ella Gladstone Martin. Pearce J. Carefoote, at the Thomas Fisher Rare Book Library in Toronto, was an eagle-eyed reader for accuracy and style who assisted in our visuals research. He and others – Professor Wesley Wark of the U. of T. Munk Centre; Giselle Byrnes of Victoria University in Wellington, Australia; Darleen Bogart at the Canadian National Institute for the Blind; Aris Babikian (the Ontario vice-president of the Armenian National Committee); Professor Ed Safarian; and author Sally Armstrong – saved me from many inadvertent errors. I'd also like to thank friend and fellow walker Mary Janigan, who first told me the story of Lucan, and who, along with her husband, Tom Kierans, has been so generous with books and ideas. Thanks, too, to John Fraser and Massey College. Leslie McGrath, at the Toronto Public Library's Osborne Collection of Early Children's Books, went out of her way to be helpful in hunting down illustration possibilities. Sakura Handa read the chapters on Shotoku and Murasaki; I will never forget her notes, criticism, and gracious encouragement. And finally, I'd like to thank my talented editor, Gena K. Gorrell, and my visuals editor, Jonathan Webb.

Index

Agrippina (mother of Emperor Nero), 19, 20-21
Alberti, Leon, 120
Alexander the Great, 9-10, 38, 116, 117
Alexandria, library at, 38
al-Mustasim, Caliph of Baghdad, 41, 42
Alphabets, 5, 14, 15, 17, 25-30;
    Armenian, 28-30, 29, 94;
    Korean (Hangul), 48-49, 51, 103;
    see also Writing
Auld family (slave-owners), 88-89, 90, 91, 92
Ayub, Ahmed, 112, 114, 118
Ayub, Nelofer, 112-18

Babington, Anthony, 63, 64, 66
Barbier de la Serre, Nicholas-Marie-Charles, 84-85
Bible, 3, 5, 28, 55-61,103;
    printed by Gutenberg, 52-53;
    translations of, 56-61, 57
bin Laden, Osama, 114, 118

Boleyn, Anne, 59, 60, 62, 66
Books: banning of, 56, 71, 71-72, 116;
    burning and destruction of, 20, 38-39, 43, 56, 60, 101, 109, 116;
    censoring of, 76-80, 101-111;
    see also Reading
Bowdler, Harriet, 78, 79-80
Bowdler, John, 78
Bowdler, Thomas, 76-78, 77
Braille, Louis, 81-86, 82

Caligula, Emperor (Rome), 20
Censorship, see Books
Cochlaeus, 56, 58
Codes and code-breaking, 14, 14, 15-16, 62-66, 119-25;
    the Enigma machine, 121, 121-23
Columbus, Christopher, 44
Comic books, 101-111;
    the Comics Code, 110
Confucius, 46, 47, 49

Dokyo, 32-33
Donenfeld, Harry, 105-106, 107,
    108-109
Douglass, Frederick, 87-93, 92, 120;
    My Bondage and My Freedom,
    91-92

Elizabeth I, Queen (England), 62, 63,
    63, 64, 66
En-hedu-anna, 5, 5-7, 116
Epic of Gilgamesh, 5
Evans, Arthur, 8-17, *11*

Family Shakspeare, The, 75, 76-80
Fujiwara no Michinaga, 36-37
Fust, Johannes, 51-52, 53

Gaines, Bill, 107, 109-110
Gaines, Charlie, 104-107
Godwin, William, 75
Gower Shad, Queen, 116-17
Gutenberg, Johannes, 45-46, 46,
    50-53, 55

Heke, Hone, 94-100, 95, 100
Henry VIII, King (England), 55,
    59-60, 63
Hitler, Adolf, 101, 106, 109
Homer, 9-12, 16, 17, 20, 28, 116

James I, King (England), 61, 63
Jami, Hakim, 118
Julius Caesar, Emperor (Rome), 19,
    20, 22, 25, 38

Kawiti, 95, 98, 99
Keller, Helen, 101
Khan, Genghis, 40, 116
Khan, Hulagu, 40-42, 41, 43-44
Khan, Kublai, 40, 43
Knossos, discovery of, 12-13, 16, 17
Kober, Alice, 15

Lamb, Charles, 74, 75-76
Lamb, Mary, 74, 75-76
Landa, Bishop, 38-39
Lessons for Children, 75
Lewis, C.S., 3
Literacy, *see* Reading
Lucan, Marcus Annaeus, 18-24
Luther, Martin, 56, 70

Mary, Queen (Scotland),62-64, 63,
    65, 66, 119, 120
Mesrob Mashtots, 26-30, 27
More, Sir Thomas, 58, 59, 60-61
Murasaki Shikibu, Lady, 34-37, 35
Mussolini, Benito, 101, 106
Mycenae, discovery of ruins at,
    10-11, 12

Nau, Claude, 62, 63
Nero, Claudius Drusus Caesar,
    Emperor (Rome), 19-24, 19
Newbery, John, 73-75

Omar, Caliph of Damascus, 38
Omar, Mullah (Mohammed), 114, 118
Orwell, George, 101, 106

Phelippes, Thomas, 64, 66
Polo, Maffeo, 43-44
Polo, Marco, 44
Polo, Niccolò, 43-44
Printing: block method, 33, 35, 43, 44, 46; movable type and mass production, 45-54, 58, 61

Raudskinna (*Redskin*), legend of, 68-70
Reading: political and religious power of, 26, 47, 51, 53-54, 55-56, 67-72, 88-93, 112-18; skill denied to certain groups, 4, 6, 7, 34, 35, 45, 53-54, 88, 103, 112-18; skill lost, 8, 16
Rejewski, Marian, 122, 123, 125
Rowling, J. K., 3, 72

Sargon I, King (Mesopotamia), 4, 6
Scherbius, Arthur, 121
Schliemann, Heinrich, 10-12, 17
Schoeffer, Peter, Jr., 55-58
Schoeffer, Peter, Sr., 51-52, 55
Sejong, King (Korea), 45-49, 50, 51, 53, 54, 103
Seneca, 20-21, 23, 24
Shakespeare, William, 3, 60; censoring of his plays, 73-80
Shi Huang-di, Emperor (China), 38
Shoshi, Empress (Japan), 34, 36
Shotoku, Empress (Japan), 31, 32-33; the "Million-Pagoda Prayers," 33

Shuster, Joe, 103-105, 108-109
Sibyl of Cumae, 1-2, *2*
Siegel, Jerry, 103-105, 106, 108-109
Superman, 101, 103, 104-106, 107-109, 110

Taejong, King (Korea), 46, 47
Tale of Genji, The, 34-37, *35*
Tales from Shakespear, 74, 75-76
Taliban, and ban on female education, 112-18, *113*
Tarquin, King (Rome), 1-2
Thousand and One Arabian Nights, The, 3, 39
Tolkien, J.R.R., 3
Translation, importance of: of aboriginal treaties, 96-100; of the Bible, 56-58, 59, 60, 103
Trojan War, legends of, 9-10
Troy, discovery of, 10-11, 17
Turing, Alan, 122, 123-24, *124*, 125
Turner, Nat, 89
Tyndale, William, 56-61, 70

Vaughan, Stephen, 59
Ventris, Michael, 14, 15-16
Vramshapouh, King (Armenia), 25, 26, 29

Walsingham, Sir Francis, 64-66, *65*
Wertham, Fredric, 108-110, *108*
Wollstonecraft, Mary, 73, 75; *A Vindication of the Rights of Women*, 73

Writing: ancient methods, 7, 12, 13;
    Braille system, 81-86;
    picture, character, and syllable
systems, 13-15, 36, 48, 49;
see also Alphabets

You Can't Read This